GREAT
BUILDING
FEATS

THE PANAMA CANAL

LESLEY A. DuTEMPLE

Lerner Publications Company
Minneapolis

For my father, with love

Lerner Publications Company
A division of Lerner Publishing Group
241 First Avenue North
Minneapolis, MN 55401

Website address: www.lernerbooks.com

Library of Congress Cataloging-in-Publication Data

DuTemple, Lesley A.
    The Panama Canal / by Lesley A. DuTemple.
        p.   cm. — (Great building feats)
    Includes bibliographical references and index.
    Summary: A history of the building of the Panama Canal, with emphasis on the difficulties of digging a canal where some engineers said it could not be done.
    ISBN: 0–8225–0079–5 (lib. bdg. : alk. paper)
    1. Panama Canal (Panama)—History—Juvenile literature. [1. Panama Canal (Panama)—History.] I. Title. II. Series.
    F1569.C2 D8 2003
    972.87'5—dc21   2001004656

Manufactured in the United States of America
2 3 4 5 6 7 – JR – 09 08 07 06 05 04

CONTENTS

ABOUT GREAT BUILDING FEATS

HUMANS HAVE LONG SOUGHT to make their mark on the world. From the ancient Great Wall of China to the ultramodern Channel Tunnel linking Great Britain and France, grand structures reveal how people have tried to express themselves and better their lives.

Great structures serve a number of purposes. Sometimes they meet a practical need. For example, the New York subway system makes getting around a huge city easier. Other structures reflect religious beliefs. The Pantheon in Rome, Italy, was created as a temple to Roman gods and later became a Catholic church. Sometimes we can only guess at the story behind a structure. The purpose of Stonehenge in England eludes us, and perhaps it always will.

This book is one in a series of books called Great Building Feats. Each book in the series takes a close look at some of the most amazing building feats around the world. Each of them posed a

For nearly a century, the Panama Canal has linked the Atlantic and Pacific Oceans, fostering world commerce and travel.

unique set of engineering and geographical problems. In many cases, these problems seemed nearly insurmountable when construction began.

More than a compilation of facts, the Great Building Feats series not only describes how each structure was built but also why. Each project called forth the best minds of its time. Many people invested their all in the outcome. Their lives are as much a part of the structure as the earth and stone used in its construction. Finally, each structure in the Great Building Feats series remains a dynamic feature of the modern world, still amazing users and viewers as well as historians.

WHY A CANAL?

The Panama Canal has a history spanning hundreds of years. Yet it also occupies a critical place in the modern world. It is a superb example of a great building feat.

The nation of Panama occupies an isthmus (a narrow strip of land that connects two larger pieces of land). The Isthmus of Panama links North and South America. Just 30 to 40 miles (48 to 64 kilometers) across, the isthmus runs mostly parallel to the equator, serving as a slight east/west detour along the mostly north/south path between the continents. It acts as a barrier between two oceans—the Atlantic (via the Caribbean Sea) on the north and the Pacific on the south.

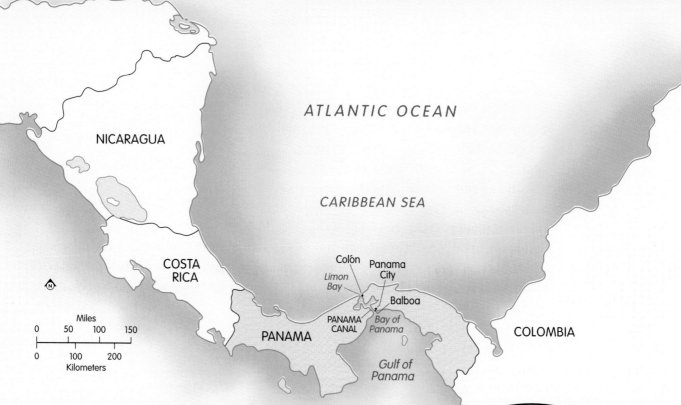

NICARAGUA

COSTA RICA

PANAMA

COLOMBIA

ATLANTIC OCEAN

CARIBBEAN SEA

Colón
Panama City
Limon Bay
Balboa
PANAMA CANAL
Bay of Panama
Gulf of Panama

PACIFIC OCEAN

Miles
0   50   100   150

0   100   200
Kilometers

People had long wanted to construct a canal through Panama. For generations, long-distance travel was mostly carried out by sea. To get from the Atlantic to the Pacific, ships had to travel around Cape Horn at the tip of South America. The two oceans come together there, creating enormous waves and treacherous storms. Besides, the trip around the cape took months. With a canal in Panama, a ship sailing from New York to San Francisco could save about 8,000 miles (12,800 km) and as much as five months of travel time.

Yet building a canal was not merely a matter of convenience. In the late nineteenth century, nations were eager to expand their power. International trade was one key to expanded power. Another key was the ability of a navy to move around the world quickly.

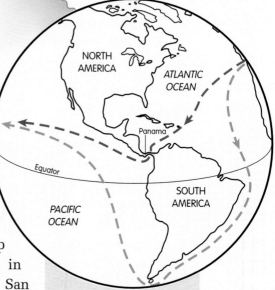

NORTH AMERICA

ATLANTIC OCEAN

Panama

Equator

SOUTH AMERICA

PACIFIC OCEAN

Panama is located on the isthmus that connects North and South America. The canal at Panama saves ships thousands of miles and months of travel time.

Planning for a canal in Panama began in 1879. The project was completed more than thirty years later at a cost of $400 million. Two nations—France and the United States—staked their national pride on the Panama Canal. Seventy-five thousand people from many different countries journeyed to Panama to work on it. An estimated one out of three of them died from accidents and tropical disease.

Yet no other single project has produced so many breakthroughs in so many fields. The canal's builders pushed the limits of their era's knowledge of electricity. Solving the problems of construction also triggered many advances in medicine, hydroengineering, geological engineering, and other fields.

At noon on December 31, 1999, the United States relinquished all rights to the Panama Canal, ceding them to the nation of Panama. The story of how the United States came to construct a canal on the soil of a sovereign nation is fascinating. So, too, is the story of how the canal's builders found solutions to the endless technical problems they faced while struggling against enormous odds.

CANALS AROUND THE WORLD

A canal is a waterway built by humans. Canals usually connect two natural bodies of water, such as lakes or oceans. Canals are often water highways for ships, shortening the distance they travel between two places. Other canals carry irrigation water for farms or divert sewage runoff. Some are used to drain swamps.

Historians think the first canal was built in 4000 B.C. in Upper Egypt by King Menes. In 600 B.C., people in China connected the Huang River and the Huai River with a canal. Canals continued to be built through the centuries. One modern canal is the Tennessee-Tombigbee Waterway in the United States, which connects the Tombigbee River in Alabama with the Tennessee River's Pickwick Lake.

Canals are found all over the world. The Netherlands, Russia, and China have many canals. In Italy, the city of Venice is built around canals. Instead of driving cars on roads, people steer boats through the canals. The longest canal in the world is the Grand Canal of China, which is 1,000 miles long (1,609 km).

Chapter One
THE PATH BETWEEN TWO OCEANS
(1492–1889)

IN 1904 U.S. PRESIDENT Theodore Roosevelt called John Findley Wallace, his newly appointed chief engineer for the Panama Canal project, into his office. The burly Roosevelt gave Wallace his orders with one terse statement: "Make the dirt fly!" Roosevelt was sending Wallace to the narrow Central American country of Panama to dig a ditch.

Wallace had never been to Panama, but he'd heard plenty of horror stories. Years earlier, a U.S. company had built a railroad across the isthmus that carried adventurers (among others) to California to join the gold rush. A legend had sprung up, told from coast to coast, that one man had died for each of the 74,000 railroad ties put in place. That story was certainly exaggerated. But, in fact, thousands of workers had died in mud slides that swallowed up entire trains, in dynamite accidents, and from disease. So making the dirt fly would be the least of Wallace's problems. He bought a coffin to take with him, "just in case."

Wallace arrived in Panama in the summer of 1904. He found, as he knew he would, some of the most difficult and dangerous terrain in the world. After just a year on the job, he was convinced that no canal could be dug there. He resigned, grateful to escape with his life.

Although the dirt would eventually fly, the price paid would be enormous. How did the building of a canal in Panama turn into the greatest project of the century? The answers stretch all the way back to Christopher Columbus.

Above, one of Columbus's ships en route to the New World. *Opposite,* Christopher Columbus and his crew landed in the Americas in 1492. Columbus made four voyages to the New World between 1492 and 1504.

SEEKING THE EAST

When Christopher Columbus first sailed from Spain in 1492, he was searching for Asia. When he landed in the Americas, he quickly realized he hadn't reached the Far East. But he was sure a great western ocean lay just beyond this strange new land.

In 1502 Columbus sailed the coast of Panama, convinced that it held the key to the mystery. He paused at the mouth of the Chagres River, where the present-day Panama Canal enters the Atlantic, to question the local people. Did they know of another sea? Yes, they did. If he would leave his ship and follow them, they would take him to it.

Columbus ordered his men to raise anchor and follow the local people as they made their way along the Chagres. They found vines and ferns, orchids glowing with color, and monkeys chattering in the treetops. When Columbus's ship could no longer make its way against the current, he switched to canoes. He and his men paddled upriver until they were finally grounded in a shallow stream.

They had arrived within 12 miles (19 km) of the western ocean. They could smell the salty ocean air. But they didn't leave their canoes and continue on foot. A stubborn man, Columbus would reach his goal by water or not at all. He never found his great western ocean.

A few years later, in September of 1513, a Spanish explorer traveled a similar path. Following local guides, Vasco Nuñez de Balboa and his crew hacked a way through stifling jungle. In mid-October, they were rewarded by seeing what Columbus knew was there, but missed seeing—the vast blue expanse of the Pacific. Balboa called it the South Sea.

Balboa and his men became the first Europeans to cross the isthmus and encounter the Pacific Ocean.

A CLOSER LOOK AT THE ISTHMUS

European explorers quickly discovered that no waterway connected the two oceans. In 1529 a Spaniard named Alvaro de Saavedra Ceron suggested digging a canal across the Isthmus of Panama. Spain was a strong military power, one of a handful of nations that sailed forth, exploring and colonizing the globe. A canal would create a valuable shipping lane for its ships.

Natural Obstacles

When Balboa crossed the Isthmus of Panama, he encountered a host of natural obstacles that later made Panama a nearly impossible site for large-scale construction.

Unyielding Mountains

The Tabasará Mountains run through central Panama like a backbone. This steep range rises to a height of nearly 5,000 feet (1,525 meters) of solid rock cliffs and slippery clay slopes. Most of Panama's many rivers originate here. A continental divide, the range funnels rivers on its eastern slopes into the Atlantic and rivers on the western side into the Pacific. Anyone crossing Panama on foot has to go over these mountains.

Unbearable Heat

Panama is warm all year round. January to April is summer, or the dry season. April through December is winter, or the rainy season. Temperatures rarely drop below 70 degrees Fahrenheit (21 degrees Celsius). They frequently rise much higher, sometimes soaring over 130 degrees Fahrenheit (55°C).

Endless Rain

Panama's long rainy season lasts for about 250 days, or more than two-thirds of the year. Massive storms soak the region with roughly 200 inches (510 centimeters) of rainwater annually. The soil, which is clay in many places, gets heavy and gooey with water.

Raging Rivers

During the rainy season, rivers in the Tabasará Mountains collect enormous amounts of rainwater as they rush downward. Large rivers can rise more than 20 feet (6 m), the height of a two-story house, in one day. One large river is the Chagres. In Balboa's time, the Chagres looped back and forth, winding like a snake on its journey to the Atlantic. During the rainy season, it could flood hundreds of acres of surrounding land.

Dense Jungles

The foothills of the Tabasarás slope out into lowlands on both the north and the south. The lowlands include fertile plains (where farmers grow bananas and sugar), marshes, and dense jungle. Jaguars, monkeys, snakes, and millions of insects inhabit the jungles. The vegetation is so thick that much of the jungle has never been explored, even in modern times.

King Charles V of Spain ordered his engineers to study explorers' reports on Panama's geography. But they advised him that Panama had too many swamps, mountains, jungles, and flooding rivers. The terrain was too rough, the project too dangerous.

Several years later, another Spanish king, Philip II, discussed the canal idea with his advisers. They reminded him that the Bible said, "What God has joined together, let no man put asunder." A god-fearing king, Philip issued a royal decree stating that anyone who tried to build a canal across the Isthmus of Panama would be put to death. Interest in the project ended.

In 1835 U.S. president Andrew Jackson sent a U.S. Army team to Panama to investigate how easily a canal could be built. After several days in the jungle, the team concluded anyone with "common or uncommon sense" could see the terrain made a canal nearly impossible to build.

The outlook for a canal in Panama did not improve after construction began on the Panama

In the centuries before roads were built on the isthmus, many travelers tried to find a way through its mountains and dense jungles. Some travelers got lost and were never seen again.

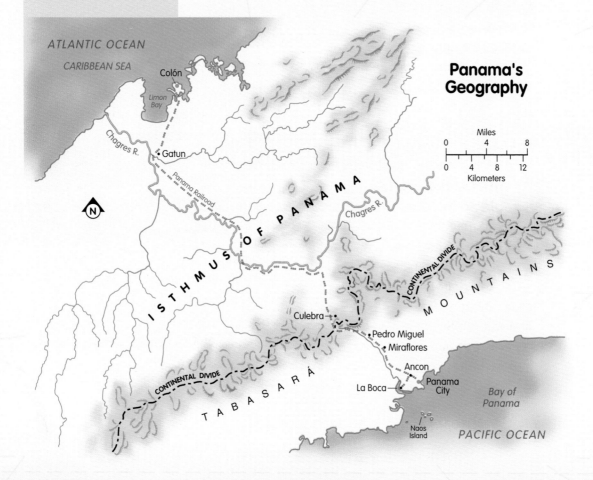

Panama's Geography

Railroad in 1850. In July 1852, a group of U.S. soldiers and their families took the train as far as it had been completed. They were on their way to duty in California. The officer in charge was Ulysses S. Grant, who later became a U.S. president. Nearly 150 men, women, and children lost their lives to cholera during that journey. Grant grieved the deaths but also saw the importance of a canal. He later recommended "an American canal" be built "on American soil."

The people of Panama had joined their neighbor Colombia in a nation known as Greater Colombia. In the 1840s, they had fought to win their independence, but lost. So it was Colombia, not Panama, that controlled the area when a group of Frenchmen decided they wanted to build a canal.

THE FRENCH
TACKLE THE ISTHMUS

By the late 1870s, the French were considered the world's foremost canal builders. They had completed the monumental Suez Canal in 1869. It connected the Mediterranean Sea and the Red Sea, considerably shortening the route between Europe and Asia. Although a private company had run the Suez project, the French government had invested more than half the money needed. French people had a sense of national pride in it.

THE PANAMA RAILROAD

When gold was discovered in California in 1848, people wanted to go west and try their luck. At the time, people used one of two routes to get to California. They could sail on a ship around Cape Horn. Or they could travel overland through largely unsettled territory. Both routes were dangerous.

By 1849 many gold miners had started taking ships to Panama. Once there, they would trek across the isthmus and catch another ship to California. To speed them on their way, a group of New York businessmen received permission from Colombia in 1850 to build a railroad across the Isthmus of Panama. It ran between Colón on the Atlantic side and Panama City on the Pacific side. During the five years it took to complete the railroad, nearly six thousand construction workers died, most from jungle diseases.

After the Panama Railroad opened, people could travel from Colón to Panama City in just four hours. A one-way ticket cost $25 in gold.

The U.S. transcontinental railroad was completed in 1869, linking the East and West Coasts of North America. People could reach California without going through Panama, and the golden days of the Panama Railroad ended.

Opening ceremonies for the Suez Canal in Egypt. Because of his successful completion of the Suez, Ferdinand de Lesseps was called the "Great Frenchman."

Many grew confident that a canal could be built in Panama. In 1879 a group of investors banded together to form the French Committee for Cutting the Interoceanic Canal. Many of them had been involved in building the Suez Canal. Ordinary French citizens felt the company represented them when it asked Colombia for permission to locate a canal in Panama.

The president and driving force behind the French Committee for Cutting the Interoceanic Canal was Ferdinand de Lesseps. He had little or no technical background, but that was not uncommon among professional builders and engineers in that era. Lesseps had been in charge of the Suez Canal project. Brilliant and determined, he appeared to be the ideal man for the job in Panama.

NOT THE SUEZ

Unfortunately, the Suez project and the Panama project had little in common. The geography and climate of the two were entirely different. For example, the terrain around the Suez was nearly level and mostly desert. Dug through dry sand that was relatively easy to handle, the Suez Canal connected two bodies of water that were almost at the same level.

The Suez Canal was dug through level, sandy ground.

Panama, on the other hand, was covered by mountains. Rain poured down for 250 days a year. The soil was slippery clay. And the tides on the Pacific side could reach 20 feet (6 m) or more, while the Caribbean (Atlantic) side had almost no tide. This meant the two bodies of water to be connected were seemingly at different levels.

But Panama and its coasts had never been thoroughly surveyed. Ill informed, Lesseps sailed to Panama and arrived during the dry season. This season brings balmy temperatures of about 80 degrees Fahrenheit (27°C). Little rain falls, and mild winds freshen everything. During Lesseps's visit, his enthusiasm for the Panama project grew.

Charles de Lesseps, Lesseps's son and a trained engineer, thought digging a canal in Panama would be nearly impossible. He tried to talk his father out of getting involved. "You succeeded at the Suez by a miracle," Charles told his father. "Be satisfied with accomplishing one miracle in a lifetime and not hope for a second."

> "You succeeded at the Suez by a miracle. Be satisfied with accomplishing one miracle in a lifetime and not hope for a second."
> —Charles de Lesseps to his father, Ferdinand de Lesseps *(shown)*

"My mind is made up," Lesseps replied. In 1879 the Colombian government gave Lesseps's company permission to build a canal. Lesseps was ready to begin.

SEA-LEVEL OR LOCK CANAL?

Lesseps already knew the kind of canal he would build: a sea-level canal like the one he had built at the Suez. To build a sea-level canal in Panama, he would need to blast a deep channel across the isthmus. The oceans on each side would then seep into the cut, creating a waterway deep enough to float the largest ship.

Most people would have been daunted by this task. In Panama's mountainous interior, the canal would need to be 300 feet deep (91 m). Workers would be using the tools of the nineteenth century—

SEA-LEVEL AND LOCK CANALS

If a canal connects two bodies of water that are at the same level, a sea-level canal can be built between them. Sea-level canals have only one level. A canal that needs more than one level includes sections called locks. Locks can move ships up and down like escalators and elevators move people.

A lock is like a watertight box big enough to hold a ship. The ship enters the lock through doors, which are then closed tight behind it. Water is poured into the lock from the higher water level. As the water level in the lock rises, so does the ship. When the water level is high enough, doors in front of the ship are opened. The ship moves out into the next level of the canal.

small and feeble compared to modern equipment—to pry apart two vast continents.

Advisers warned Lesseps against a sea-level canal. A sea-level canal cut through the mountains would have sides so steep that they would collapse. On the other hand, a lock system could carry ships up and over the steep passes of the mountains. A lock canal's channel would need to be only about 85 feet deep (26 m).

But Lesseps held firm to the idea of a sea-level canal. Having conquered the Suez, he may have believed he could put a sea-level canal anywhere. Dynamite could certainly slice a deep cut through the mountains, he thought. Besides, the Suez Canal was 100 miles long (160 km). The one in Panama would be only 30 to 50 miles long (48 to 80 km)—a piece of cake.

WHICH ROUTE?

Lesseps also had to think about what route the canal should take. One German naturalist, Alexander von Humboldt, had identified five possible routes between the Atlantic and Pacific Oceans. Von Humboldt favored a route across Nicaragua rather than Panama.

But Lesseps realized that his crews would be excavating huge piles of spoil (earth and rock that would need to be removed after being dug or blasted out of the way). Trains would be needed to haul it out of the way. The best route would be that of the Panama Railroad. It was the shortest way across Panama.

Again, advisers cautioned Lesseps against his plan, especially if he remained committed to a sea-level canal. The railroad route was short, but it climbed along the highest mountain peaks. In addition, the Chagres River crossed the

The Panama Railroad traversed the isthmus. It climbed along Panama's steeply sloping mountains—a difficult route for a sea-level canal.

tracks at several places and often flooded them. On the other hand, if Lesseps built a lock canal, the railway route might work. Locks could carry ships up the steeply climbing path of the railroad. For reasons known only to himself, Lesseps steadfastly insisted on a sea-level canal along the railway route. He was so committed that he bought the rights to the railroad.

The canal would begin at the city of Colón on the Atlantic coast. It would angle across the isthmus through the mountains in Panama's interior and onward to Panama City on the Pacific. The Atlantic entrance would be northwest of the Pacific entrance. Channels would have to be dug in the bays at both entrances to allow oceangoing vessels to approach shore. And something would have to be done about the Chagres. Lesseps would need an estimated $130 million to do the job. "He can get the money," predicted the *New York Tribune,* "and unquestionably he has the genius requisite for surmounting the engineering difficulties."

Panama itself could not supply enough workers for the massive project. So Lesseps recruited workers from nearby Caribbean islands (then called the West Indies). Lesseps also recruited in the United States, in Europe, and in other places around the world. Hundreds of men signed on, prepared to live and work for years, miles away from home.

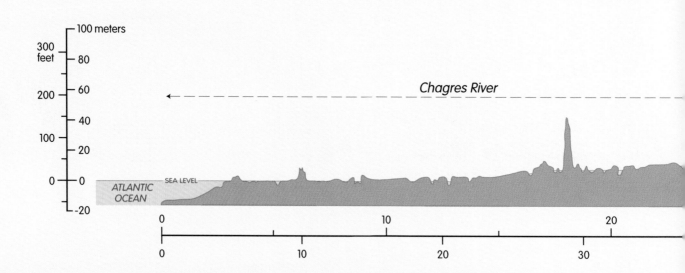

RUST, MOLD, AND CLAY

When canal workers arrived in Panama, they took up stations at various work sites along the projected route. Lesseps divided the work into three main excavations: the ship canal and two channels to divert water from the Chagres River. By the end of 1881, two thousand men were at work on these projects.

The weather became a problem almost immediately. Lesseps's crews found themselves in pouring rain. The waterlogged clay soil turned heavy and

Above, laborers at work on the Panama Canal. Muddy, wet conditions and irregular terrain presented many problems.

Below, a cross section of Panama before construction of the canal. The cross section has been condensed to fit on this page. The mountains in Panama have gradual slopes, not sharp, vertical slopes as shown here.

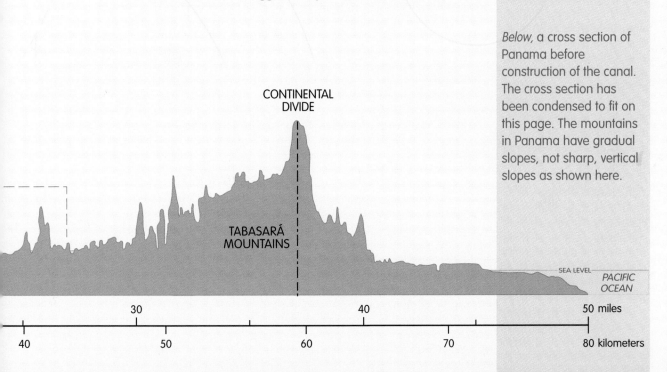

CONTINENTAL DIVIDE

TABASARÁ MOUNTAINS

SEA LEVEL

PACIFIC OCEAN

30   40   50 miles

40   50   60   70   80 kilometers

THE PROBLEM OF MACHINES

To excavate, Lesseps's company used Slaven dredging machines made in the United States. The dredging machines were 120 feet (36 m) wide and 70 feet (21 m) tall. Steam engines hauled buckets of spoil to the top of one of these dredging machines, which dumped it down a chute 180 feet (55 m) long. As enormous as these machines were, they were not big enough to handle the job. Workers often had to struggle for hours to move boulders that were too large and too heavy for their equipment.

gooey, sticking to the scoops of the steam shovels. Workers had to shovel off the clay by hand. The wild Chagres River flooded and caused mud slides in areas that had been cleared. Temperatures soared. In the damp heat, mold grew on workers' shoes overnight. Machinery rusted in less than a week.

Meanwhile, Lesseps was making mistakes. He didn't have a blueprint, and he was disorganized in other ways as well. He had workers lay down new sections of railroad track with a gauge that didn't match the existing track.

A French crew churns away at the hillside, removing spoil.

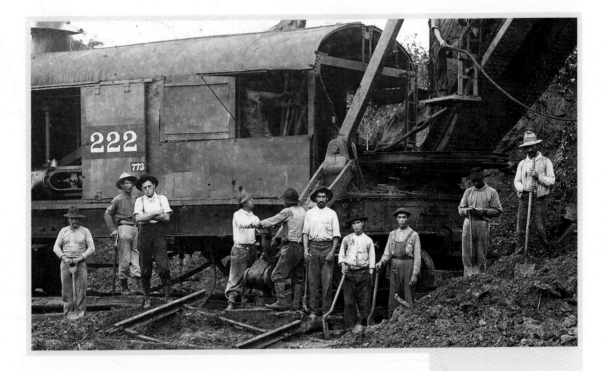

Another problem was that the company didn't have enough money. Lesseps had used an optimistic estimate of the funds that would be needed, and he quickly ran short of cash. Since he couldn't afford good housing for his workers, they were living in rough wooden shacks with no screens on the windows. Insects swarmed into the shacks every night. As one worker wrote home, insects would swarm around a candle so thickly that their bodies would extinguish the flame. Yet there was nowhere else to go but home when the day's tasks were finished. The area had no restaurants, theaters, or any kind of entertainment. Lesseps traveled constantly, trying to raise funds, but he could never raise enough. His workers had to struggle along with their inadequate housing, rusted equipment, and not enough tools. All these things were enough to dishearten the most cheerful worker. But even worse than lack of money, rain, mud slides, and swarming insects was . . . disease.

One of the French company's crews pauses for a photo. Living and working conditions in Panama were poor.

The death certificate of a twenty-nine-year-old Frenchman, 1886. He died of yellow fever, which took the lives of hundreds of workers.

"THE WHITE MAN'S GRAVEYARD"

Lesseps's men fell ill with yellow fever, malaria, and other tropical diseases at an alarming rate. Black workers got sick just as much as white workers did. But many people believed that white people were more vulnerable, calling Panama the white man's graveyard.

Malaria was an ever-present threat. A medicine called quinine helped prevent it. People who fell ill with malaria grew feverish, with shivering so intense it could shake a room. Survivors experienced recurrences of the disease again and again, months and even years afterward.

Yellow fever killed fewer people than malaria did. "But it was a far more violent and hideous thing to see; a more gruesome way to die," as historian David McCullough put it. Victims of yellow fever suffered a high fever and searing headaches, turned yellow, and spit up a blackish vomit. Survivors became immune. But only half of the victims survived.

Yellow fever attacked in epidemic waves during the rainy season, then receded again. One French engineer told of arriving in Colón with seventeen other young Frenchmen. Within a month, he was the only man alive. During some periods, ships bobbed at anchor in Colón harbor with no living soul aboard.

In that era, no one understood what caused these diseases. Doctors had few medicines or other treatments with which to help those who got sick. An astonishing one in five workers died of illness— two hundred a month in some periods. Ferdinand de Lesseps, who played down the "supposed deadliness" of the isthmus, gained the nickname the Great Undertaker.

> Yellow fever killed fewer people than malaria did. But death by yellow fever "was a far more violent and hideous thing to see."
>
> —historian David McCullough

To make matters worse, in 1882 an earthquake struck Panama. In many places where the canal had been excavated, the earthquake sent mud sliding down the canal walls. Many sections filled in. The railroad line sank 10 feet (3 m) in places. Lesseps's company was right back where it had started. By 1885, almost four years after work began, only one-tenth of the estimated excavation had been completed.

DEFEATED BY THE ISTHMUS

Ferdinand de Lesseps was rarely in Panama. As work on the canal inched along over the next years, he was able to ignore the obvious: his project was in big trouble. Finally, his own company refused to advance any more money unless he changed to a lock canal. Only then did Lesseps reluctantly abandon his dream of a sea-level canal.

But it was too late. By 1889 Lesseps's workers had excavated 30,000,000 cubic yards of earth (23,000,000 cubic meters) in several locations along the proposed route. Lesseps's company had spent

The French canal company abandoned this equipment—and much more—when it left Panama in defeat. At home some Frenchmen accused the company not only of failing to build the canal but also of cheating investors.

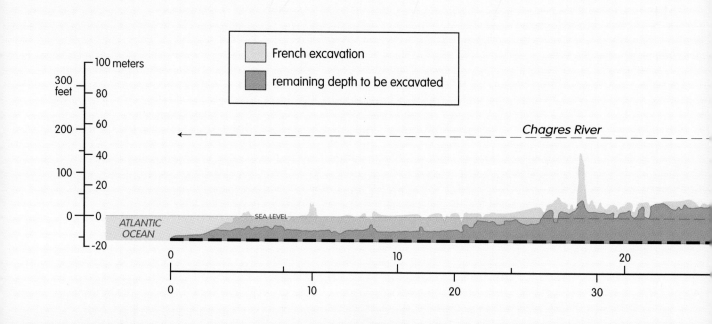

French excavation

remaining depth to be excavated

Chagres River

100 meters
300 feet
80

200 60

40

100 20

0 0

SEA LEVEL

-20

ATLANTIC OCEAN

0   10   20

0   10   20   30

$287 million of investors' money—more than double the original estimate. Lesseps was unable to raise any more money. Not even the French government would help.

Ten years after starting the Panama Canal, Lesseps's company closed down the project. Ferdinand de Lesseps returned to France, shut himself in his house, and mourned his failure. Outraged investors took him to court, and he was found guilty of fraud. He never had to go to jail, but his reputation was ruined. "The shame of it drove the old man . . . insane," according to writer Arthur Bullard in one of the earliest memoirs of Panama. Lesseps died five years later, a heartbroken man.

Left behind in Panama were many pieces of rusting equipment, abandoned on hillsides and in swamps; a few empty hospitals; and many, many cemeteries where thousands of workers lay buried. For a decade, the world had eagerly watched Ferdinand de Lesseps trying to dig a canal in Panama. If he couldn't do it, who could? Perhaps the Atlantic and Pacific Oceans were destined to remain separated by Panama forever.

This cross section of Panama in 1889 gives some idea of how little excavation the French had achieved in ten years. To create a sea-level canal, the French company would have had to dig down below sea level—as far as the thick dashed line—a long way to go.

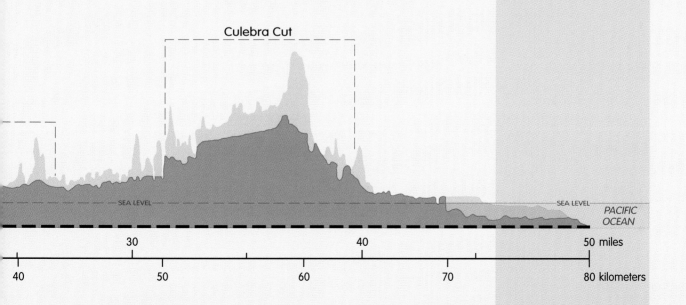

Culebra Cut

SEA LEVEL

SEA LEVEL
PACIFIC OCEAN

30   40   50 miles
40   50   60   70   80 kilometers

Chapter Two
THE UNITED STATES AND PANAMA
(1889-1904)

WHEN LESSEPS'S COMPANY went bankrupt in 1889, all digging in Panama stopped. The company reorganized as the French New Panama Canal Company and kept a few employees. Their job was to find a buyer for the canal project so investors could recover some of their money. For many years, the company searched in vain. Then in 1898, an unexpected buyer showed up.

THE SPANISH-AMERICAN WAR

In 1898 war broke out between the United States and Spain over events occurring in Cuba, an island nation in the Caribbean that was under Spain's control. The Cubans were fighting for independence. To aid

Above, it took more than two months for the USS *Oregon* to sail from California to Cuba. *Opposite,* Teddy Roosevelt as a Rough Rider during the Spanish-American War.

them, the U.S. Navy ordered one of its largest battleships, the USS *Oregon,* to Cuba. The only problem was that the *Oregon* was in San Francisco, 12,000 miles (19,308 km) and one ocean away.

The *Oregon* made its way toward Cuba as quickly as possible and finally arrived in Cuba sixty-seven days later. By then, Americans were alarmed at how long it had taken for the needed help to arrive. If full-speed, emergency trips took so long, how could the United States ever defend its two ocean borders? Many Americans began clamoring for a canal across the isthmus.

The loudest voice was that of Theodore Roosevelt, who was the nation's assistant secretary of the navy. Eager to join the war in Cuba, he resigned from his position and formed a group of volunteer soldiers called the Rough Riders. Roosevelt led the Rough Riders to spectacular victories in Cuba. The experience showed him that his youthful nation could become a world power someday. To do that, though, it had to be able to aid its allies and defend its borders effectively. A Central American canal was vital to those goals.

Three years later, Roosevelt became president of the United States. One of his first goals was to get Congress to approve the building of a canal. Another effort by a private company would fail, he believed, so the project must be undertaken by the government. In his first address to Congress on December 3, 1901, he declared, "No single great material work which remains to be undertaken on this continent is of such consequence to the American people."

ENTER PHILIPPE BUNAU-VARILLA

Sensing a golden opportunity, the French canal company promptly offered to sell its Panamanian rights to Congress for $100 million. Many congressmen supported the idea of a canal but favored Nicaragua as a site.

Philippe Bunau-Varilla journeyed to the United States in 1902 to try to convince Congress to buy the rights to the Panama route.

As Congress hotly debated the proposed canal in Panama, Philippe Bunau-Varilla, a French engineer, began lobbying vigorously for it. He had invested over $400 thousand in the French canal project and was determined to recoup at least some of his losses.

First, Bunau-Varilla wrote and printed thirteen thousand copies of a pamphlet entitled *Panama or Nicaragua?* that said Nicaragua was dangerous because of its volcanoes. Bunau-Varilla distributed the pamphlet not only to congressmen but also to governors, bankers, ship owners, and newspaper editors.

Then, just three days before Congress was to vote on the purchase of the Panama rights, Bunau-Varilla sent copies of a Nicaraguan postage stamp to every member. It showed a volcano about to erupt. Bunau-Varilla attached the following message: "An official witness of the volcanic activity

"PANAMA . . . OR NICARAGUA?"

Some members of Congress wanted a canal, but they wanted one in Nicaragua, not Panama. Three congressional commissions (in 1895, 1897, and 1899) had investigated several possible routes. All three commissions had recommended Nicaragua instead of Panama.

A Nicaraguan canal would be closer to the United States by several hundred miles. The lowest point in the mountain chain that runs through Central America is in Nicaragua. There was less disease in Nicaragua. Several navigable rivers and a large lake already existed. If these things weren't enough, the United States already had six treaties with Nicaragua giving it permission to build a canal there.

So why Panama? Lobbying efforts by Philippe Bunau-Varilla and others were largely responsible. Roosevelt also wanted a canal in Panama, and he was a powerful man. In spite of all its known difficulties, the Panama route won.

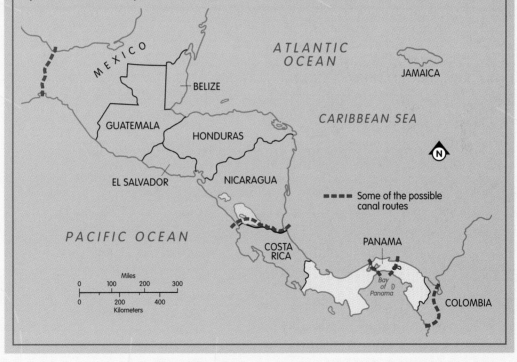

on the isthmus of Nicaragua." It didn't matter that nearly every volcano in Nicaragua was extinct.

In the end, Congress did vote to build a canal in Panama, and the French company accepted its offer of $40 million. The right to build in

Panama now belonged to the United States of America . . . sort of.

DEALING WITH COLOMBIA

One important detail remained. The French company's original contract with Colombia stated that the Colombian government had the right to approve or disapprove construction of a canal in Panama by anyone other than the French company. And the United States was no favorite with Colombia or other Latin American countries. Many of them believed the United States should not have been involved in the Spanish-American War.

After much negotiation with Colombia, the U.S. Senate approved a canal treaty in 1903. But then the Colombian government refused to approve it. Roosevelt was furious. He decided to take matters into his own hands.

Panama had long been wanting independence from Colombia. In 1903 tensions were high. Panama wanted to negotiate directly with the United States but needed its independence to do so. Through Bunau-Varilla and his agents in Panama, Roosevelt

Below, Panama's coast. Colombia controlled Panama when the United States tried to negotiate a canal treaty in 1903.

let it be known that if the Panamanians wanted to revolt, the United States would offer assistance.

Bunau-Varilla quickly organized a revolution. Given the history of tension between Panama and Colombia, his job was not difficult. Many Panamanians quickly joined his cause. He worked closely with Roosevelt, keeping the president informed every step of the way.

On October 30, 1903, acting under Roosevelt's orders, an American gunboat, the USS *Nashville,* steamed into Panama's harbor. A second gunboat followed two days later. On November 3, 1903, with two U.S. gunboats standing by to protect them, the Panamanians revolted. Bunau-Varilla had written a declaration of independence for them. As rebellious Panamanians took to the streets, Roosevelt ordered the Panama Railroad not to transport Colombian troops.

> On October 30, 1903, acting under Roosevelt's orders, an American gunboat, the USS *Nashville,* steamed into Panama's harbor.

The *Nashville* and a Colombian gunboat trained their guns on each other, but neither fired. Colombia was too weak to challenge U.S. power, and no real fighting occurred. Three days after the revolution started, the Colombians simply went home. Only one person had died—a Chinese shopkeeper, killed by a stray bullet.

After the revolution, representatives of Panama's new government traveled to Washington, D.C. But they were too late. The United States had already signed a treaty negotiated on behalf of Panama by Philippe Bunau-Varilla. Bunau-Varilla had not even consulted Panama's leaders.

Bunau-Varilla recovered his entire investment and even made some profit. For the rest of his life, he maintained that he had acted like any patriotic Frenchman. He had served France and avenged its honor.

DEALING WITH PANAMA

When the United States formally recognized the Republic of Panama on November 6, 1903, people immediately raised an outcry. In the eyes of many people around the world, the United States had clearly overstepped its bounds by preventing Colombia from putting down a revolution in one of its own provinces. Even in the United States, newspapers attacked Roosevelt for his "gunboat diplomacy."

> "I took the canal zone and let Congress debate."
> —President Teddy Roosevelt

The treaty that allowed the United States to build a canal across the isthmus came to be known as the Hay-Bunau-Varilla Treaty after the treaty's chief negotiators (John Hay was U.S. secretary of state). According to its terms, the United States paid Panama $10 million immediately. It would also pay $250,000 annually for the canal right-of-way. The annual payments would start nine years after the canal opened.

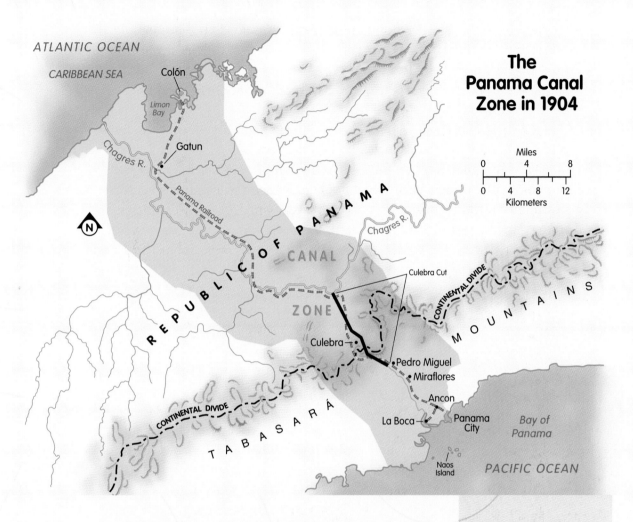

The Panama Canal Zone in 1904

ATLANTIC OCEAN

CARIBBEAN SEA

Colón

Limon Bay

Gatun

Chagres R.

Panama Railroad

REPUBLIC OF PANAMA

CANAL

ZONE

Chagres R.

Culebra Cut

CONTINENTAL DIVIDE

MOUNTAINS

Culebra

Pedro Miguel

Miraflores

Ancon

La Boca

Panama City

Bay of Panama

Naos Island

PACIFIC OCEAN

CONTINENTAL DIVIDE

TABASARÁ

N

Miles
0 4 8
0 4 8 12
Kilometers

In return, the United States was free to construct a canal across Panama. The canal would be built within a swath of land 10 miles (16 km) wide from coast to coast. The Panama Canal Zone (or the zone, as the area was called) would be controlled by the United States. The United States was also granted four islands in the Bay of Panama and the right to take over any land or water "necessary and convenient" for the construction, operation, maintenance, sanitation, or protection of the canal.

This map shows the strip of land reserved for the Panama Canal Zone. When negotiations with Colombia failed to give the United States the right to build here, Roosevelt took military action to gain the right-of-way.

Chapter Three
ONE CANAL ... THREE ENGINEERS
(1904-1907)

WITH PANAMA HIS, ROOSEVELT got down to the business of canal construction. He appointed an Isthmian Canal Commission of seven men to administer the project. By June 1904, they had chosen John Findley Wallace, a respected railroad engineer, as chief engineer. Only Roosevelt himself had a higher government salary than the $25,000 a year Wallace would receive.

Wallace and the seven commissioners arrived in Panama on July 1, 1904. They found an enormous mess. At canal headquarters in Panama City, the unpaved streets were ankle-deep in sewage and mud. The wrecks of rusted machinery and about two thousand ruined offices, warehouses, and dwellings littered the zone. Rats, termites, mold, and insects were everywhere.

The French had begun dredging the harbors, but had sunk eighty dredging machines and numerous tugboats when they left. The French

The first U.S. crews in Panama salvaged some French equipment, such as these hand cars.

had also begun cutting through the mountains in the interior and had excavated several miles of canal near Colón. Between these points were miles of land as yet untouched.

When the commissioners returned to Washington, D.C., one month later, Wallace was left with the mess. He hardly knew where to begin. But then six French machine shops and a power plant were found to be in working order. Wallace's men salvaged the dredges and tugboats from the harbor and repaired them. They also renovated some of the buildings left by the French. Although no decision had been made about whether to build a sea-level or lock canal (Congress couldn't decide), Wallace started digging.

"THE BRAIN"

Almost immediately, Wallace found himself frustrated. The commission imposed such strict guidelines for ordering supplies that it was nearly impossible to get anything. It took months for goods to arrive in Panama, and when they did, they were often the wrong items. One shipment even contained snow shovels.

Then there was the problem of Wallace himself. He should have drawn up a complete plan for adequate housing and food for the thousands of workers needed to do the job. Instead, he concentrated on beginning excavation with the limited equipment and men he had.

And Wallace had no ability to get along with people. Instead of communicating with workers, he rode around in a small locomotive. He never got out. He only looked. Workers scornfully called his train the Brain's Car.

By November 1904, 3,500 workers were living in the zone, nearly all of them men. (In fact, fewer than three hundred women were employed during the entire construction of the canal.) Most men lived in ramshackle, unscreened barracks. They had no refrigeration for their food and no sanitation system. "Everybody is afflicted with running sores," worker Charles Carroll wrote to his mother in Pennsylvania. "The meals would sicken a dog." "There is not a bit of amusement or pleasure of the remotest kind here," another worker wrote in a letter to the *New York Herald.* "It is a case of work, work, work, all day long, and infrequently all night long, with no reward in view."

John Findley Wallace, *above,* largely ignored the counsel of Dr. William Gorgas, the canal's chief medical officer.

Wallace also should have tackled the problem of disease. The commission had appointed Dr. William Gorgas as chief medical officer. Gorgas had become the leading American authority on tropical diseases after wiping out malaria and yellow fever in Cuba. He knew that mosquitoes carried both diseases. Eliminate the mosquitoes, and you eliminate the disease. But convincing ordinary people of this was not easy.

Wallace himself found it difficult to believe that killing mosquitoes would end disease. Like many people of this era, he believed that fever victims got sick from drinking too much alcohol and other bad habits. Panama posed no health threat, he said, to any "clean, healthy, moral American."

To fund Gorgas's controversial work, the commission provided a meager budget of $50,000. Wallace gave Gorgas only a limited staff. When Gorgas begged architect M. O. Johnson to install screens in workers' housing, Johnson said he was too busy with "important things."

An ill worker is loaded onto an ambulance. Yellow fever, malaria, and other tropical diseases took the lives of many workers and frightened away still more from Panama.

As a result, illness was rampant. In a yellow fever epidemic in 1905, many members of Wallace's staff died, one after the other. When architect Johnson died, he was buried in Wallace's casket.

Workers fled. "A . . . man's a fool to go there and a bigger fool to stay," worker Harry Brainard declared when he returned home to Albany, New York. Then on July 3, one man died of bubonic plague. Panama didn't have enough boats to carry away workers after that. Nearly three-quarters of American workers left, unwilling to endure the conditions.

Wallace cabled U.S. secretary of war William Howard Taft, asking permission to travel to the United States to discuss urgent business. When the two met, Wallace had nothing to say about disease in Panama. Instead, he announced that he was considering accepting another job. He indicated he might be persuaded to stay on if he was given more money, made commission chairman, and given full control of all work.

Taft was appalled. "You come with the bald announcement that you quit your task at a critical moment," he snapped. Taft was "inexpressibly disappointed" and ordered Wallace to resign. Within one month, a new chief engineer was on his way to Panama.

"THE BIG SMOKE"

Like Wallace, John Frank Stevens was a railroad man. Unlike Wallace, he had started his career as a laborer and worked his way up, proving his worth to railroad tycoon James J. Hill by locating an important pass through the mountains of present-day Glacier National Park. He had discovered the pass on foot and alone, in subzero temperatures, and became a legend in the West. "I learned to adapt myself . . . under the most primitive conditions," Stevens said later. "And I loved it!" Roosevelt told his son Kermit that the broad-shouldered Stevens was "a big fellow, a man of daring and good sense."

Clearly, Stevens was not easily daunted. When he arrived in Panama in July 1905, he found a pile of coffins on the dock awaiting use and ambulances taking yellow fever patients to the hospital. His first order was that all digging stop. The key to survival lay in planning. "The most important stage in any great undertaking is the preparatory stage," he announced. "The digging is the least of all."

John Frank Stevens constructed houses, hospitals, and schools, creating communities that would attract—and keep—skilled workers in the Panama Canal Zone.

As a first step, Stevens began building complete communities of houses, hospitals, schools, and water and sewage systems. He wanted a stable working force, so he encouraged workers to send for their families. Some women were thrilled to join their husbands. "Lord, yes, I liked it here," said one young teacher. "I didn't know anything else but the hills of West Virginia."

Black workers fared less well than white workers. They were segregated into separate housing, separate hospitals, and separate schools for their children. Most facilities for blacks were inferior to those for whites. Most white workers were skilled American craftsmen, while most black workers were unskilled laborers from the Caribbean.

Above, a gang of workers pitches in to construct a sewer system in Colón.

Left, bathers head to the beach at Limon Bay near Colón. Under Stevens, canal employees were encouraged to bring their wives and families to Panama to make the years spent working on the canal more tolerable.

Above, typical housing for black laborers. Most workers on the Panama Canal were black. Many came from nearby islands in the Caribbean.

Stevens rubbed shoulders with everyone. He knew how to do every job and tramped along the line every day, talking to the men and checking every detail—always puffing on a big cigar. He was never without that cigar, so the workers began calling him Big Smoke.

Stevens also grasped the single greatest logistical problem of the project (which neither Wallace nor the French had ever understood). Digging was pointless when workers had no way to move the dirt well out of the way. Within a year, Stevens rebuilt the rusty, broken-down Panama Railroad (which still ran alongside the proposed canal route). He had new track laid and ordered state-of-the-art locomotives and railroad cars. Even with all this equipment, however, one major obstacle remained. Stevens needed to keep his workers alive.

FIGHTING DISEASE

Perhaps the most remarkable difference between Wallace and Stevens was the support Stevens threw behind Dr. William Gorgas. While Gorgas's previous budget had been paltry, under Stevens money was no object. Stevens assigned four thousand workers to Gorgas and ordered that their work be given top priority.

Gorgas started the biggest, most expensive sanitation program the world had ever seen. First, he ordered that ships docking in Panama be checked for signs of disease. If necessary, a ship was fumigated and the passengers were quarantined.

The mosquitoes that transmit yellow fever live around humans. So Gorgas had nearly every room in every building in the zone fumigated and screened. He ordered $90,000 worth of copper screening alone. His most stunning purchase was 120 tons (122 metric tons) of insect powder—the entire U.S. output for one year. His crews cleared away brush and undergrowth and sprayed insecticide wherever people were working or living.

Since mosquitoes breed on standing water, the crews sprayed kerosene on all standing water. Gorgas even ordered that containers that might collect standing water be destroyed. "Colonel Gorgas has been described as a man with a gentle manner but a hard policy toward mosquitoes," one woman living in Panama reported. Using these exhaustive methods, Gorgas eliminated yellow fever in less than a year.

Malaria is carried by a different type of mosquito, one that breeds throughout the jungle, not just near people. Many black workers lived in unscreened shacks scattered in remote jungle areas. So malaria was harder to control, and it continued to take a higher toll than all other diseases combined. All the same, the number of reported cases began to drop.

Dr. William Gorgas, *above*, helped to wage a campaign in Panama against mosquitoes and the diseases they carry. *Right,* a worker in Panama applies insecticide on standing water, where mosquitoes could breed.

One young worker, James A. Williams of Jamaica, was a kitchen assistant when he came down with a fever. "The Doctor immediately advanced to me and felt my pulse," James later wrote. "He said to me you are going to die." James, a teenager who had never been in a hospital, was sent to the hospital in the village of Ancon. He was diagnosed with malaria until doctors realized he had typhoid. At one point, "two men came with a Stretcher and lifted me from the bed. . . . I thought they were going to bury me," James wrote. James survived, in part thanks to "those American Nurses." People continued to get sick in Panama. But the improvement in worker health was great enough that workers were willing to come to the zone and stay.

THE PLAN

The canal would be dug over the narrowest part of the isthmus. It would cut deeply into the mountains in Panama's interior near the town of Culebra, taking advantage of some of the work the French had done. The plan also continued the excavation begun by the French on the Pacific side. On the Atlantic side, however, Stevens would follow an entirely new route.

Congress finally approved a lock canal in the summer of 1906. Stevens's design called for several sets of locks. It also included several dams. The largest would dam the Chagres River to create a huge artificial lake—Gatun Lake. The other dams would create smaller lakes.

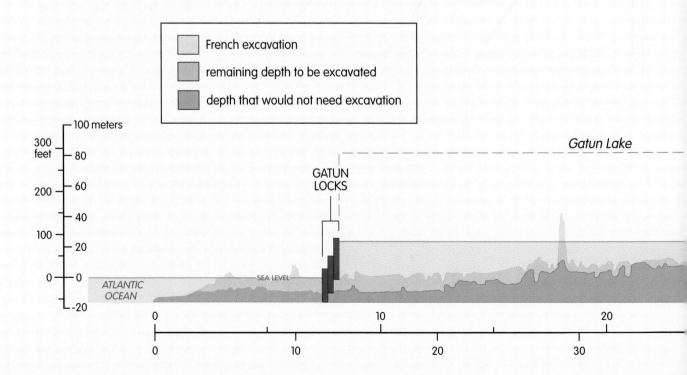

LET CONGRESS DECIDE

For nearly two years, Congress wavered between building a sea-level canal and building a lock canal. To choose, members of Congress had to study a confusing pile of reports. Roosevelt summarized the main facts of the reports in a letter dated February 19, 1906. "The sea-level canal would be slightly less exposed to damage in the event of war," he wrote. A sea-level canal would also be cheaper to maintain.

On the other hand, a lock canal would cost only half as much and "could be built in about half the time," Roosevelt wrote. There would be "very much less risk connected with building it." Finally, "after being built, it would be easier to enlarge."

Although Roosevelt advised a lock canal, he would honor whatever plan Congress adopted, he said. Not surprisingly, Congress approved a lock canal that June.

To use the canal, ships coming from the Atlantic would approach Panama's coast at Limon Bay, near the town of Colón. A deep-water channel would be dredged to enable ships to sail into the entrance to the canal. From there, the canal would take them inland to the village of Gatun. The first set of locks would be located at Gatun. The locks would raise ships in three flights to Gatun Lake.

Under the U.S. plan, locks at both the Atlantic and Pacific ends would carry ships up a long, elevated waterway. If the United States could excavate all the terrain shown in dark gray, the canal would have the required minimum depth of 85 feet (26 m) throughout.

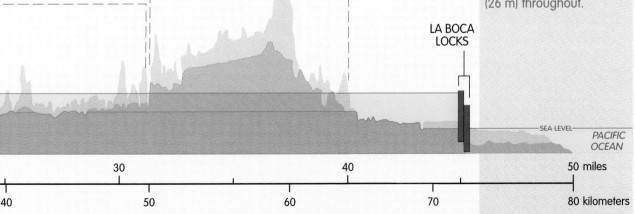

Culebra Cut

LA BOCA
LOCKS

SEA LEVEL

PACIFIC
OCEAN

30   40   50 miles

40   50   60   70   80 kilometers

After crossing Gatun Lake, ships would enter Culebra Cut, a deep channel that would take them through the mountains. At the southern end of Culebra Cut, ships would enter locks at the village of La Boca. Another deep-water channel would be dredged in the Bay of Panama to allow ships to sail out to the deep water of the Pacific Ocean. In all, the voyage would be about 50 miles (80 km) long and would take ten to twelve hours. Inland rivers would provide all the water needed to fill the canal with water and to run the locks. With adequate living conditions provided for most workers and a solid plan in place, the dirt was truly flying by November 1906. Roosevelt decided it was time to pay a visit to the zone.

"A REAL PLEASURE TO LOOK AT THEM"

Becoming the first U.S. president ever to set foot on foreign soil as president, Roosevelt journeyed to Panama and tramped around for three days. "We worked from morning till night," he wrote to his son Kermit. He asked countless questions, tried out equipment, and wore everyone out with his boundless energy.

He wanted to mingle with ordinary workers, so he ate nearly every meal with them. In Culebra Cut, he found a steam shovel crew. They'd hastily hung a banner that read WE WILL DO OUR BEST TO HELP YOU DIG IT. Roosevelt shook hands with each of the men. "I am immensely struck by the character of American employees," he told Kermit. "From the top to the bottom these men are so hardy, so efficient, so energetic, that it is a real pleasure to look at them."

Canal workers thronged to meet President Teddy Roosevelt, *at center, in white suit,* when he visited the canal in 1906.

Everything he saw seemed to inspire him. He raved about Panama's "real tropic forest, palms and bananas, . . . gorgeous butterflies and brilliant colored birds." When he returned home, he was more convinced than ever that the canal in Panama was "an epic feat, and one of immense significance."

He had been particularly pleased with Stevens, even though Stevens couldn't keep up with him. ("I have blisters on both feet and am worn out," Stevens had said to get out of one excursion with Roosevelt.) So Roosevelt was shocked to get a letter from Stevens in February 1906 coldly stating, "To me the canal is only a big ditch. . . . Possibly I lack imagination." When Stevens hinted that he had better things to do, the president

> "From the top to the bottom these men are so hardy, so efficient, so energetic, that it is a real pleasure to look at them."
>
> —President Teddy Roosevelt

took the hint to mean that Stevens was resigning. Roosevelt sent the letter to Taft with a note saying, "Stevens must get out at once."

Whether Stevens resigned or was fired, he did leave Panama. Thousands of workers came to the dock to say good-bye to him. They presented him with a gold watch, diamond ring, silver tea set, and two bound volumes containing the signatures of more than ten thousand employees.

Having lost two engineers in three years, Roosevelt vowed that he would not lose another. He would put the canal "in charge of men who will stay on the job . . . till I say they may abandon it." The only men Roosevelt could control in that way were in the military.

"THE OLD MAN"

In February 1907, Roosevelt appointed Lieutenant Colonel George Washington Goethals of the U.S. Army to be the new chief engineer of the Panama Canal. "I am ordered down," Goethals wrote to a friend. "There is no alternative."

He did have an alternative, since Roosevelt took him out of the army for this assignment. But like most army men, Goethals had the habit of

Five workers relax after a long day's work. The fellow second from left reads an issue of the *Canal Record,* a weekly newsletter published by Goethals.

following the orders of his commanding officer. Roosevelt, tired of committees, said Goethals would be the highest authority in Panama and would report—not to the commission—but directly to him and the secretary of war.

Goethals arrived in the zone in March 1907. "I am commanding the Army of Panama, and the enemy we are going to combat is the Culebra Cut and the locks and dams at both ends of the canal," he told workers. But these workers were not soldiers. They were civilians who had come to Panama to make money, and they could leave at any time. Many of them bristled at the mention of the army. Besides, Big Smoke was a tough act to follow. Goethals did not get a warm reception. Many people on his staff resigned almost immediately.

Eventually Goethals found ways to communicate with people. After a few months on the job, he began publishing a weekly newsletter, the *Canal Record.* It was filled with information about the canal, social events, the price of food—anything that would be of interest to "zonians."

Goethals also began holding open meetings every Sunday morning where workers could come to his house with complaints or problems.

"Once in a while," Goethals explained, "something turns up which is really important for me to know." Many began calling him the Old Man.

Goethals also reorganized the Panama Canal Zone into three divisions and assigned a head engineer to each. Sydney B. Williamson was in charge of the Pacific Division. David Gaillard headed the Central Division. And William Sibert directed the Atlantic Division.

Ill-equipped to gain people's affection the way Stevens had, Goethals nonetheless won the respect of the workers. His excellent judgment, skill, and fairness were hard to ignore. "The Old Man is straight as a string," one worker commented, "and the men are strong for him. You could go a long way—all the way—and not find a better boss."

THE TEN-DOLLAR MOSQUITO

Gorgas and Goethals never developed a friendly working relationship, especially when Goethals (in an effort to save money) decided to assume responsibility for all brush clearing. Gorgas claimed this decision stopped him from eliminating malaria from the zone. But Goethals got the work done much more cheaply.

Mrs. Gorgas described Goethals as humorless and dictatorial. According to her, Goethals had once told Gorgas, "Do you know, Gorgas, that every mosquito you kill costs the United States Government ten dollars?" Gorgas had replied, "But just think, one of those ten-dollar mosquitoes might bite you, and what a loss that would be to the country."

Goethals, *first row at center, in white suit,* accompanied by his crew, including William Sibert, *far left,* William Gorgas, *second from right,* and David Gaillard, *far right.*

Chapter Four
THE CULEBRA CUT
(1907–1913)

OF THE THREE DIVISIONS Goethals had organized, the most challenging was the Central Division headed by David Gaillard. It contained Culebra Cut. In Spanish, *culebra* means "snake." *Cut* is an engineering term for a human-made ditch. The Culebra Cut was going to be a steep-sided ditch that snaked its way for 9 miles (14.5 km) through the mountains of Panama's interior. Not surprisingly, the cut also came to be called Hell's Gorge.

Ships would pass directly from Culebra Cut into Gatun Lake, so the water level of the canal in the cut had to match the water level of the lake. The cut would have to be dug 45 feet (14 m) below the surface of the lake to create a channel deep enough for ships to navigate safely. This meant digging down the height of a four-story apartment building. The French had started digging at Culebra, but they had barely scratched the surface.

Above, a massive steam shovel loads rock. *Right,* excavating Culebra Cut was a seemingly endless task.

Culebra Cut was the "Big Job." Within one year of Goethals's arrival, the cut swarmed with activity and screeching noise. Workers scurried, drills shrieked as they bit through rock, shovels puffed and dug, and trains continuously rumbled along the tracks. An average of thirty-seven steam shovels worked in the cut at all times, and two hundred dirt trains ran back and forth every day.

Arthur Bullard, a traveler and writer, described standing on a high point and looking down into the cut. "One glance down into the . . . abyss and you will realize that those midgets of men are not doing the work," he wrote. "They are only arranging it for the monsters of steel whose food is fire and whose breath is steam and black smoke. . . . Through all the long day you can hear them roaring and shrieking over their prey."

At night, when the digging crews went home, maintenance workers repaired and refueled the equipment. Blasting crews set off dynamite charges. Trains scuttled back and forth from the cut so that everything would be ready the next morning. There were no nine-to-five workdays, no weekends off. Crews rotated constantly, and the railroad ran twenty-four hours a day.

Dynamite crews worked under the constant threat of deadly accidents.

THE DYNAMITE DETAIL

Because the cut went through rocky mountains, blasting with dynamite was the key to the whole excavation. Goethals assigned six thousand workers to the Central Division. Of these, Gaillard assigned nearly half to the dynamite detail.

To be effective, the dynamite had to be placed deep within the rock. Workers drilled holes as much as 27 feet deep (8 m). With as many as three hundred drills going at once, the noise in Culebra Cut was deafening. Drilling took place all hours of the day.

The blasting was done only when the main workers weren't around, usually at night or during the lunch hour. Arthur Bullard was having tea with some of the supervisors' wives one day when he heard "a grumble of thunder, a quiver of earth, and my chair jumped half an inch." He spilled his scalding hot tea on his knee. "What was that?" he asked nervously. "Oh," his hostess told him, "that's nothing. They always shoot at five o'clock." She meant that the dynamite men were blasting away, "using more dynamite in a week than the rest of the world uses in a month," by Bullard's estimate.

Dynamite was unpredictable, and working with it was one of the most dangerous jobs in the zone. No matter how careful the crews were, accidents happened. Sometimes explosions went off too soon. Sometimes lightning hit the charges. Human error also caused many accidents.

The worst disaster occurred December 12, 1908, when 44,000 pounds (19,976 kilograms) of dynamite loaded into fifty-two holes went off unexpectedly. As a Caribbean worker recounted, "You see bits of men here and a head yonder. Oh, they were picking it up for days. Oh, boy! That wasn't an easy day, I tell you." No one could discover the cause of the accident. Despite the dangers of blasting, there was nothing to do but continue. Blasting was the only way to clear the cut.

MOVING IT OUT

Dynamiting knocked down the mountains, but that was only the beginning. Once the mountain mud and rock were blasted, the debris, or spoil, had to be cleared away.

At Culebra, the mountains were cut into terraces. Steam shovels sat on their own set of tracks on a lower terrace, with their scoops pointing into the hill. Gaillard divided the shovels into two main groups and stationed one at each end of the cut. The goal was for the two groups to meet in the middle.

The steam shovels were Bucyrus steam shovels that could scoop up 8 tons (7.3 metric tons) of spoil in a single swing—three to five times as much as the machines used by the French. So Gaillard expected faster progress than the French had made. One

The Americans gradually replaced the older, smaller French equipment with state-of-the art equipment such as this huge Bucyrus steam shovel.

A dirt train waits on a track above a steam shovel.

visitor said the energetic Bucyrus steam shovels would look just like Theodore Roosevelt "if they only wore glasses."

Above the steam shovels, on a different terrace and on different tracks, were the dirt trains. Each dirt train was twenty cars long. A steel sheet covered the floor and ran the entire length of twenty cars, making an ultra-long boxcar.

The steam shovels worked constantly to load spoil into the dirt trains. When one dirt train was loaded, another pulled into its place. Because the steam shovels dug down and toward the middle, to keep working, both sets of tracks were continually moved. Special crews did nothing but move tracks.

As each dirt train left the cut, yard masters directed it. There were sixty different dumping grounds within 20 miles (32 km). The dumps were huge, some of them covering as much as 1,000 acres (405 hectares).

With hundreds of trains and thousands of workers, the cut appeared to be nothing but chaos and booming noise. But it was actually a tightly controlled area. Gaillard was a master scheduler, and he made sure that no crew—or project—ever interfered with another.

BREAKING THE BACK OF THE ISTHMUS

Like the French company workers, Gaillard's men found that rain posed a considerable challenge. In 1909 Panama reported 237 inches (602 cm) of rain, compared to 50 inches (127 cm) that fell in Washington, D.C., the same year. The rain was followed by heat reaching 103 degrees Fahrenheit (39°C).

Even without rain, Culebra Cut was a mucky mess. Small streams trickled into the work area, and groundwater seeped upward from deep underground. Gaillard built dikes and diversion channels, but still the water came.

When the sides of the cut began caving in, the landslides were "wet" slides. One huge wet slide shoved more than 50 acres (20 hectares) of mud to the bottom of the cut. Gaillard described the mess as a "tropical glacier of mud instead of ice." Workers spent more than a month clearing just this one slide.

As the cut deepened, cracks formed in the walls. The weight of the cliffs on top caused the ground at the bottom to push upward. Sometimes the floor of the canal

A Sliding Town

In 1910 most of the entire town of Culebra gradually slid into the cut. The slide didn't move fast—only about 3 feet (1 m) a day. Gaillard tried to stop the slide by building concrete retaining walls. But the concrete walls simply started sliding along with everything else. "The neighbors three doors east of us were warned time and again that it was not safe to stay," one young mother wrote about neighbors who would not leave town. "One morning they awakened to find their back steps well on the way to the bottom of the cut."

Eventually the division headquarters, two rows of worker cottages, the zone's largest YMCA, a jail, and other buildings all had to be torn down and rebuilt in another location. All told, more than 75 acres (30 hectares) disappeared into Culebra Cut.

Pressure from the steeply sloping sides of Culebra Cut sometimes forced the ground at the bottom to buckle, wreaking havoc with railroad tracks.

silently rose 10 or even 20 feet (3 to 6 m). Once Gaillard was astonished to see a steam shovel sinking before his eyes. Then he realized that the shovel wasn't sinking—the ground he was standing on was rising. In these unstable conditions, whole sections came crumbling down in "dry" landslides.

Clearing slides, wet or dry, took a lot of time and set the work schedule behind. In 1911 Gaillard spent three months just removing slides from the cut. In 1912 moving slides out of the way took four months.

The original French excavation had widened the top of the cut to 670 feet (204 m), or about as wide as two football fields are long. As the Americans worked, the top had reached a width of 840 feet (256 m). In desperation, Goethals and Gaillard decided to widen the top of the cut still more, to 1,800 feet (549 m), or about as wide as five and a half football fields are long. Instead of having sharply sloping sides, the cut would have gently sloping sides.

It seemed the Big Job would never end. As one worker from Barbados put it, "I personally [believed that] my children would come and have children, and their children would come and do the same, before you would see water in the Cut." Slowly, however, the cut deepened as the steam shovels gnawed away at the mountains, day after day.

Then in early 1913, a massive slide covered the bottom of the cut and moved more than 60 feet (18 m) up the opposite side. Clearly, angling the sides was not going to stop all slides. In shock, Gaillard

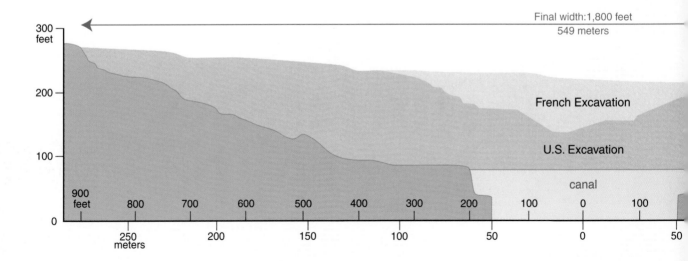

asked Goethals what to do. Goethals had seen near-ly everything Panama could dish out by then. He just looked at Gaillard and replied, "H——, dig it out again."

Above, dredges clear a giant mud slide at the bottom of Culebra Cut in 1913.

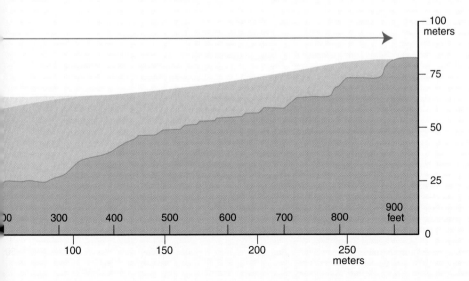

Left, this cross section shows how much U.S. engineers widened Culebra Cut, creating gently sloping sides that would prevent mud slides. The final width in 1914 was approximately 1,800 feet (549 m).

Chapter Five
TAMING THE CHAGRES
(1907–1913)

Workers in the zone pause atop a dirt train's load.

AS WORKERS STRUGGLED WITH the challenges of Culebra Cut, others were confronting another difficulty at least as great: the meandering and powerful Chagres River. The Chagres originates high in the mountains in central Panama and flows downward to the Atlantic. On its 120-mile (192-km) journey, the Chagres crossed the proposed canal route twenty-two times.

During the rainy season, the Chagres filled so rapidly with so much water that it sometimes rose 20 feet (6 m) in a single day, overflowing its banks and flooding the surrounding area, sometimes for miles. Its power and unpredictability clearly threatened construction efforts. "The one great problem in the construction of [the] canal . . . is the control of the Chagres River," John Stevens had insisted. "That overshadows everything else." And the only way to control the Chagres was to dam it.

GETTING READY

The plans called for an earthen dam across the Chagres near the village of Gatun, about 4 miles (6.4 km) inland from the Atlantic. At that point, the river flowed through a narrow valley lined by low, rocky hills. The dam would stretch for 1.5 miles (2.4 km) across the valley. At its base, the dam would be 0.25 mile (0.4 km) thick. It would stand 100 feet (30 m) high.

Blocked by this "mountain of earth," as historian David McCullough described the dam, the Chagres would back up for miles. The resulting artificial lake would be 23 miles (7 m) long—the largest human-made lake in the world at that time. If this plan worked, the Chagres would supply the lake with water, and the lake would supply the canal with water.

To form the outside walls of the earthen dam, workers would dump huge piles of rock across the valley 0.25 mile (0.4 km) apart. Then they would fill the gap with spoil.

This plan looked plausible. But the Chagres had been choosing its own path across Panama for centuries. Goethals

A view of the Chagres River before the construction of Gatun Dam. The Panama Railroad is in the foreground, and the town of Gatun is on the facing bank.

knew that dumping a gigantic earthen dam in its way would not be easy.

The potential difficulties concerned other people as well. The enormous pressure of the water in such a huge artificial lake worried many. Some said the dam might not be watertight. Others argued that the site wasn't suitable. Supposedly the area had no solid bedrock to support the enormous dam.

Besides, people remembered the Johnstown Flood that occurred in Pennsylvania when a similar earthen dam gave way in 1889. One witness watched, horrified, as a train on an iron bridge was blasted away by the sudden flood, followed by the collapse of the bridge itself. In the town of Johnstown, below the dam, two thousand people were killed. Not surprisingly, when the plans for the Gatun Dam were made public, many Americans raised an outcry.

Goethals appointed William Sibert to head the construction of the dam. Sibert had a scale model built, then used it to demonstrate that the dam could stand the stress of water pushing against it. If the water behind the dam got too high, a concrete spillway in the middle of the dam could be opened to let some water escape.

Sibert also ordered the drilling of hundreds of test holes and test pits to make sure the soil was stable enough to support the dam. All the tests indicated the proposed dam would work just fine.

Still, the uproar in the United States continued. So Roosevelt sent six expert men, including three engineers and U.S. secretary of war William Howard Taft, to Panama to check out the Gatun Dam site.

The weather there was hot. One young soldier assigned to greet Taft commented, "Boy! You know, that place when it rains, it's just like throwing water on a stove, everything steams . . . .

William Howard Taft, *right,* visiting the zone

And here's Taft [who was a very heavy man], with a big white suit on." The committee toured everything, even venturing 87 feet (27 km) down into the test pits. They concluded that the dam would be structurally safe.

Another important step was surveying the area. Most of the river's side channels to the east of Gatun would be filled in. This would force the river water to the west. The river channels there would be widened and deepened to handle the extra water. Surveying parties tramped the jungle to identify the area that would eventually become

Gatun Lake. Some of the parties spent a year slowly cutting their way along the future lake's shoreline.

BUILDING GATUN DAM

To construct Gatun Dam, two rock retaining walls were built across the width of the valley about 0.25 mile (0.4 km) apart. The Chagres River continued to flow through an 80-foot (24-m) wide channel kept open in the middle of the valley.

Sibert first built high railroad trestles where the rock retaining walls would be. Trains pulling cars filled with broken rock traveled the trestles, then dumped their loads on either side of the trestles. Gradually the rock piles grew higher.

The weight of the newly deposited rocks caused the ground to shift constantly. This day-to-day shifting kept knocking the railroad tracks out of line, and workers had to move the track constantly (a phenomenon Sibert had expected).

When the top of the rock piles reached the top of the trestles, Sibert moved the railroad tracks off the trestles and onto the rock wall and kept dumping. Both retaining walls were finished by the spring of 1909.

Workers next filled the yawning gaps between the rock retaining walls with a soupy mixture of sand, clay, and mud. The water and lighter materials in the soupy mixture drained away through drainpipes. Heavier materials sank to the bottom. Once the heavier materials settled, dry spoil (most of it from Culebra Cut) was dumped on top. The weight of the spoil squeezed out the last water from the soupy

ALARMING NEWS

On November 21, 1908, a reporter wandered over to the Gatun Dam site and saw that a portion of the retaining wall had sunk 20 feet (6 m). The Chagres River had flooded the railroad tracks on top. Convinced that he had stumbled onto a sensational story, the reporter wrote that Gatun Dam was being built on an underground lake. All over the globe, headlines declared: "Gatun Dam Is Said To Have Sunk 60 Feet."

The headline was obviously far-fetched, especially since the dam hadn't even been built. But Goethals had to field an onslaught of questions anyway. And he hadn't even been told about the daily shifting and settling. In addition, a thoroughly annoyed President Roosevelt was forced to send yet another committee to Panama to investigate. Again, the committee approved the dam design.

mixture. Over time, the resulting earthen barricade became as hard as concrete.

Construction of the concrete spillway dam began in 1909. Regulating the flow of the river here would regulate the water level of the entire canal. When complete, it would be 808 feet (246 m) across and soar 69 feet (21 m) tall—nearly as tall as a seven-story apartment building.

While construction of the concrete spillway dam was under way, Sibert also directed several other projects. Upriver from the dam, the Chagres was still a large and unpredictable river that would change the water level in Gatun Lake quickly at times. To keep an eye on it, Sibert built a series of observation towers along its banks and along the smaller rivers that fed into it. From the towers, observers phoned dam operators regularly to report river conditions. That way, dam operators had warning if a flood was approaching.

Dry spoil from Culebra Cut. The earthen dam at Gatun was partly built with spoil from Culebra and other sites.

Workers at Gatun Dam stayed in tent camps until more permanent housing could be built.

Another major project was clearing the area. Otherwise, once the area was flooded, ships might run into submerged trees. After Culebra Cut and Gatun Dam, clearing trees should have been easy, but it wasn't. The area was so full of wildlife that workers had to be always on their guard. Monkeys constantly shrieked at them and interfered. One crew was even attacked by a jaguar. Some of the clearing was done with dynamite, and again, accidents occurred. When the area was finally cleared, the workers were nervous wrecks.

POWERING THE ZONE

As the spillway was under construction, Goethals began erecting a hydroelectric power plant next to it. Water coming from Gatun Lake would fall over the spillway into three huge pipes, drop 75 feet (23 m), and hit a giant turbine at the bottom of each pipe. The pressure of the water would turn the turbines to generate electricity.

Once the Gatun hydroelectric power plant was fully operational, it would generate all the power needed in the zone. It could power the canal locks, cranes, cement mixers, rock crushers, lighthouses, and every village and town in the zone. At the time, electricity was a brand-new invention. Many homes in the United States had no electricity at all. So an all-electric canal was quite an accomplishment. Much of the credit went to a young company that got the major contracts for the electrical work—General Electric.

By the spring of 1910, nearly everything but the concrete spillway dam was completed. The retaining walls and earthen dam were in place. It was time to close the dam.

THE CHAGRES BECOMES A LAKE

Sibert planned to complete the damming of the Chagres the same way he had built up the earthen dam's rock retaining wall—by using trains to dump rock. This time, however, workers would have to dump the rock directly in the river's path.

DISPLACED PEOPLE

Besides dealing with technical problems and public objections, Goethals had other worries when it came to Gatun Dam. When the dam was finally finished, Gatun Lake would flood several miles of the newly repaired Panama Railroad, many of the worker communities that Stevens had built, and a dozen native villages. All of these would have to be relocated.

Moving the railroad and worker communities posed no real problem. Moving native villages was another matter. According to the terms of the canal treaty, the United States owned the zone and could do what it wanted. But the villagers did not want to leave their lifelong homes. Unfortunately, neither Sibert nor Goethals ever sympathized with their viewpoint. Ultimately, the villagers were relocated against their will.

Most Panamanians were not happy with the fact that a foreign country owned a swath of Panama 10 miles (16 km) wide. The relocation of native people, from land their ancestors had occupied for centuries, sparked a riot in Panama City in 1912.

On April 22, 1910, Sibert gave the order to begin, and the trains began dumping. As rocks tumbled into the river, the walls slowly began to rise. Unfortunately, the river also began to rise, and the raging torrent began washing half-ton rocks downstream. As Sibert said later, "It looked as if the Chagres were to be the winner in the fight."

He quickly directed a train to dump carloads of rusted railroad tracks into the river, hoping that the rocks would catch in the twisted metal and hold. It was a desperate gamble. If the rusted tracks didn't hold the rocks, they would tear out the trestle, toppling the train into the river.

Minutes later, the force of the river shoved rocks and tracks into the trestle, moving it 5 feet (1.5 m) downstream with a terrible screeching sound and nearly toppling it. Heedless of the danger, the train crew scrambled down the bank and struggled to add supports to the trestle. They were able to secure it. Sibert then ordered more rock to be dumped into the river. This time, the tracks and rocks held. The Chagres River was dammed—for the moment.

Ten days later, water burst through the western section of the dam, collapsing a trestle and washing out thousands of tons of spoil. Although Sibert's crew moved quickly, they needed more than a week to repair the damage. By May the river was controlled, and the western portion of Gatun Lake was filling up.

Gradually the concrete spillway dam also took shape. A horseshoe-shaped structure, its outside curve faced Gatun Lake, and its inside

In 1910 Sibert ordered workers to dump old railroad tracks into a washout. Here workers have piled abandoned vehicles and other junk to fill a gap.

curve faced downstream. Fourteen steel gates set into the concrete opened and closed like windows to control the water flow from the lake. Any water released went into the concrete spillway first and then flowed back into the Chagres River (on the other side of the dam) and onward to the Atlantic Ocean.

The concrete spillway dam at Gatun is shaped like a horseshoe.

Lush tropical growth quickly covered the earthen dam, making it look like a jungle slope at the end of the lake. What appeared to be small islands dotting the surface of the enormous lake were the tops of hills that were all but submerged.

For all the controversy that had swirled around Gatun Dam, it turned out to be the most trouble-free undertaking of the whole Panama Canal project. It took nearly four years for the lake to fill entirely, but when it did, the force of the raging Chagres was absorbed by the placid waters of Gatun Lake. While previously the Chagres had threatened the entire canal, it now supplied the means to sustain the canal.

Chapter Six
SCULPTING BAYS AND BUILDING LOCKS
(1906–1913)

PEOPLE IN THE UNITED STATES and Europe always knew what was going on in the Central Division at Culebra Cut. Gatun Dam in the Atlantic Division also got plenty of publicity. But reporters tended to pay less attention to other projects—some of them equally amazing.

LIMON BAY

Like most bays, Limon Bay on the Atlantic coast becomes shallow near shore. Large ships crossing the bay to enter the canal would run aground unless a shipping channel (a deepwater trough) was dredged. The channel would need to continue inland from the shore for about 3 miles (5 km). At that point, ships would enter the Gatun Locks.

The work of creating the channel was done from floating barges except in one small rocky section, which had to be cleared with dynamite and steam shovels. The difference between high and low tide on the Atlantic was only 1 foot (0.3 m), which helped make the dredging relatively easy.

Above, railroad lines in Colón. *Right,* the Atlantic entrance to the canal, near Colón

Limon Bay needed to be protected by a breakwater (an offshore structure) to shield it from fierce Atlantic storms and to keep sand and silt from washing into the canal entrance. The Limon Bay breakwater would run from the shoreline out into the bay for 2 miles (3 km).

To build it, crews dumped tons of stone into the sea from barges. Then pilings, or sturdy poles, were driven into the stone, and railroad tracks were built on top. From the railroad tracks, more stone was dumped into the Atlantic, and the breakwater gradually took shape. A second, shorter breakwater was also built to further protect the harbor.

BLUNDERS AT THE PACIFIC END

The Pacific Division had no spectacular projects, so it never really captured the public interest. Even so, the Pacific Division was nagged by problems from start to finish. It was responsible for constructing the Pacific Ocean entrance to the canal. The first problem encountered was the actual site. Congress had approved a plan that called for two sets of locks on the shoreline at La Boca, and a shipping channel extending 4 miles (6 km) out into the Pacific.

Stevens had argued against La Boca. He had called for the locks to be located inland at Miraflores. But since Congress had approved the La Boca site, Goethals was forced to use that location.

With so much water in the area, construction was impossible until dams could be built. After serving as dikes during construction, the dams would help control canal water levels and operate the locks.

As soon as Goethals built railroad trestles to get construction trains into the area, the pilings settled so drastically that one train plunged right over the side. Any rock the trains managed to dump sank into the muck and caused huge humps of earth to rise up in different areas. The ground at La Boca was like a giant toothpaste tube. If you pushed on one area, the ground squished up in another place. Sometimes the ground continued rising two weeks after rocks had been dumped.

Goethals immediately ordered more test pits dug and borings drilled. Every test indicated that the soil was slippery blue clay, incapable of supporting any structure, let alone dams and locks.

The only way to fix the problem was to move the site. Given all the other problems on the Panama Canal, getting Congress to approve a new site was the last thing Goethals wanted to tackle.

Instead of taking the question to Congress, Goethals and Roosevelt simply sorted out the problem themselves. On December 20, 1907, Roosevelt sent a letter confirming Goethals's decision to move the Pacific Division locks from La Boca to Miraflores. Amazingly, no newspaper reporter picked up on the change. Members of Congress were away on Christmas vacation, and the change escaped their attention as well.

With the new location, a ship coming from the Pacific Ocean would travel a channel 8.5 miles (13.6 km) long to the two Miraflores Locks. The locks would raise the ship 55 feet (88 km) to Miraflores Lake. After crossing the mile-and-a-half-long (2.4-km) human-made lake, the Pedro Miguel Locks would raise the ship another 30 feet (9 m) to the Culebra Cut.

As at the abandoned La Boca site, two dams had to be built at each lock location (Pedro Miguel and Miraflores) to keep water out of the area during construction and eventually to operate the locks. Earthen dams also had to be built across the path of the inland channel to keep out the high tide. Although constructing the dikes was a lot of work, the effort paid off. No major problems occurred at either lock site.

THE NAOS BREAKWATER

While channels and dams were being constructed, a huge breakwater was being built in the Bay of Panama on the Pacific Ocean. It ran from

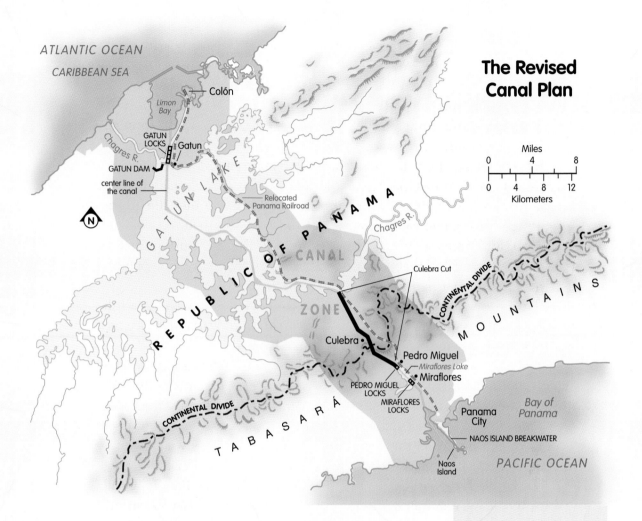

The Revised Canal Plan

ATLANTIC OCEAN

CARIBBEAN SEA

Colón

Limon Bay

GATUN LOCKS

Chagres R.

Gatun

GATUN DAM

center line of the canal

GATUN LAKE

Relocated Panama Railroad

Chagres R.

REPUBLIC OF PANAMA

CANAL

ZONE

Culebra Cut

CONTINENTAL DIVIDE

MOUNTAINS

Culebra

Pedro Miguel

Miraflores Lake

Miraflores

PEDRO MIGUEL LOCKS

MIRAFLORES LOCKS

Panama City

Bay of Panama

NAOS ISLAND BREAKWATER

Naos Island

PACIFIC OCEAN

CONTINENTAL DIVIDE

TABASARÁ

Miles

0   4   8

0   4   8   12

Kilometers

N

the entrance of the canal (at the original La Boca site), 3 miles (5 km) across the bay to Naos Island.

To build the breakwater, Goethals built train trestles across the bay as he had at Limon Bay in the Atlantic. Trains would dump rocks into the water and the breakwater would build up.

But as soon as the trestles were constructed, the project ran into the same problems that had plagued the La Boca lock site. The greasy blue clay would support nothing. The trestles toppled over and any rocks that actually got dumped caused huge hummocks to rise up in other areas.

Goethals had been able to move the locks. But he couldn't move the canal entrance. Neither could he leave the entrance unprotected from the strong Pacific currents that dumped tons of sand and silt in the bay.

Goethals's plan called for locks at Pedro Miguel and Miraflores.

The Naos breakwater in 1910

Goethals had little choice but to keep adding more spoil to stabilize the situation.

More than three years after he started, not one trestle was in its original place and the breakwater was still one mile (1.6 km) short of Naos Island. It took ten times more spoil than Goethals had originally estimated to get the Naos breakwater finished. The breakwater then served as a bridge between the mainland and Naos, Flamenco, and Perico Islands.

A MOVING ZONE

As construction on the dams, dredging, and breakwaters neared completion, the entire zone was consumed with a flurry of moving. Gatun Dam would cause the greatest flooding, but other dams would also flood areas of the zone. Everything had to be moved.

The greatest moving project was the Panama Railroad. The entire rail system needed to be moved without disrupting any of the traffic. Every day more than six hundred trains moved dirt, supplies, money, mail, freight, and passengers all over the zone. Dirt trains had the right of way over any train except a train in which the president of the United States might be riding. It took more than five years and $9 million to move the Panama Railroad out of the canal's path.

Moving everything was tedious yet exciting, because it meant the canal was nearing completion. Amid all the movement, Goethals started the last grand project of the Panama Canal: the building of the locks.

BUILDING THE LOCKS

Locks were critical to the success of the canal, and thousands of workers were assigned to the project. They set about constructing a series of locks in three locations. A set of locks in three flights would be located at Gatun. Another set of locks in two flights would be needed at Miraflores. A final lock was planned at Pedro Miguel.

Each lock would have two chambers so that two ships could be locked through at the same time. When finished, each lock would be as long as five city blocks and be taller than a six-story building. The workers spent the first two years on the locks just excavating their locations.

Crews clear the site for the Miraflores Locks.

SACRED SAND AND EXPENSIVE CEMENT

Millions of tons of sand, rock, and cement were used to build the locks. Both the sand and the rock were quarried locally. The rock was crushed into gravel at two large crushing plants in the zone. The engineers had found perfect quality sand on the nearby San Blas Islands in the Atlantic. They offered to buy it, but the Cuna Indian chief living there believed that everything on the islands was a gift from God. He refused to sell the sand—especially to white men—so the sand was quarried in Panama.

More than 4.5 million barrels of cement were used in the locks. The dry cement mixture for all of it had to be shipped in bags from the United States. Each time a bag was opened, workers shook it out thoroughly to glean every possible ounce of dry mixture. As bag after bag was opened, this step alone resulted in a savings of an estimated $50 thousand worth of material.

EXPERIMENTING WITH CONCRETE

The engineers of that era had built locks before, but no one had ever attempted anything like these giants. Many of the design principles and building techniques needed to build them had never been tried before. For example, no one had ever built such massive structures out of concrete.

Concrete is made by mixing sand, gravel, and cement together with water. The cement used in the Panama Canal locks was portland cement (a mixture of clay and limestone). Concrete was not a new building material in this era. But it had been mostly used in basements and floors. Larger concrete structures, such as small concrete bridges, were reinforced with metal bars embedded in them. Goethals decided to use nonreinforced concrete.

The locks at Gatun would stand between Gatun Lake and the rest of the canal. If the locks gave way, the lake would rush uncontrollably down into the canal. The concrete in the locks had to be strong enough to withstand the pressure of all that water in a climate where building materials, including concrete, tended to crumble quickly. The canal's engineers had to select exactly the right ratio of materials needed to form a concrete this strong. And massive quantities of it would have to be poured.

At each location, piles of sand, gravel, and cement sat next to the lock site. Because the locks would be so gigantic, a whole system had to be constructed just to mix these ingredients. The Gatun site was in an

Workers load concrete at a plant at Gatun. No earlier construction project had used concrete on such a massive scale.

open area, but the Pedro Miguel and Miraflores sites were in small valleys. Different mixing, transporting, and pouring systems had to be designed for the open site and the narrow sites. But all the locks were built in 36-foot (11-m) sections from concrete shaped in steel molds.

At Gatun, electric railcars traveled on tracks between the piles of materials, picking up the correct amounts of sand, gravel, and cement. Then the railcars delivered the materials to huge buckets that were also set on tracks. Water was then mixed into the materials by electric cement mixers. Next, an enormous overhead cable system swung the buckets with the concrete mixture and poured the concrete into the steel molds. Men stood in the molds, knee-deep in wet concrete, smoothing and spreading the mixture. Since both the steel molds and the cable-bucket system were on tracks, both setups could be moved forward when a section was finished.

This system worked well at Gatun, but the Pedro Miguel and Miraflores sites were too narrow to allow railcars to shuttle back and forth to the piles of materials. Instead, giant cranes sat on tracks on the edge of the canal. An operator swung the bucket of the crane around to a pile of materials close at hand. The bucket gathered up the correct mix

Giant cranes hover over construction at the narrow site of the Pedro Miguel Locks.

of sand, gravel, and cement, then dumped it into another giant bucket where water was added. Then the crane picked up the bucket with the concrete mixture and hooked it onto an overhead trolley system. The bucket traveled on the trolley and emptied into a mold. When a section was completed, everything moved forward to the next section.

A WATERTIGHT BOX

Gatun Lake was the main source of water for all the locks. Because the lake was 85 feet (26 m) above sea level, all the locks operated through gravity. By simply opening a valve, an operator could send water flowing down into the lock system.

Each lock was really just a giant box that held fresh water—approximately 52 million gallons (197 million liters) of it—about one day's worth of water for a midsize city. All that water couldn't be allowed to gush into the locks, because the force might damage them.

Huge culverts (pipes) were installed to control the way water entered a lock. The main culverts were 18 feet (5.5 m) in diameter—large enough for a railroad car to pass through. A system of smaller culverts connected with the main culverts. The smaller culverts ran under the

This worker is dwarfed by the huge culvert under construction at the Gatun Locks.

floor of the lock. From there, water could bubble up gently into the lock through holes drilled in the floor. After a ship had passed through the lock, a single valve would reverse the system and drain the water.

LOCK GATES

Ships would enter and exit the locks through watertight gates at each end. The gates were like double doors that swung open and shut by parting in the middle. The framework of each gate was formed with steel girders, like a giant erector set. Then steel plates were riveted, or drilled, to the girders. The gate doors ended up being hollow on the inside and completely watertight.

Each door of the gate stood 65 feet (20 m) tall, was 7 feet (2 m) thick, and weighed hundreds of tons. Each door attached to the lock wall with two hinges. The hinges alone weighed 14 tons (12.7 metric tons) each, or about as much as seven automobiles. In spite of their enormous size, the gates could be opened and closed in just two minutes, using only a 40 horse-power electric motor. That's a smaller motor than most water-ski boats use.

Not all ships were five city blocks long. To conserve water when a smaller ship was using a lock, each lock had intermediary gates built inside. By using these gates, a lock could be shortened from 1,000 feet to 600 feet (305 to 183 m), requiring less water to fill up.

Above, a gate at Gatun
Locks. The true size of the
locks—and their gates—
would be hidden once the
canal filled with water.
Below, this cross section
shows the Panama Canal
in 1913. At its completion, it
included three sets of locks.

CONTROLLING THE LOCKS

The three sets of locks (Gatun, Miraflores, and
Pedro Miguel) were controlled and operated with
hydroelectric power. Most of the electricity came
from the main power plant at Gatun Dam. The controls for each lock were housed in a building on the

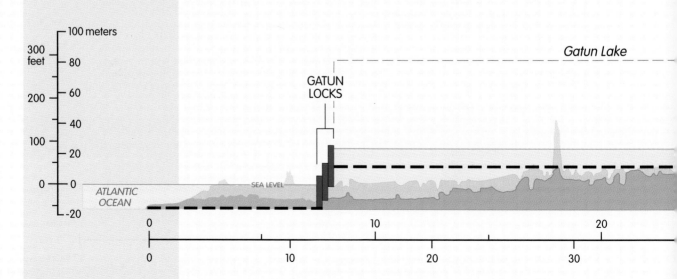

100 meters

300 feet

80

200

60

40

100

20

0

0

-20

ATLANTIC
OCEAN

SEA LEVEL

GATUN
LOCKS

Gatun Lake

0

10

20

0

10

20

30

center wall of the lock. Each set of locks had its own building and set of controls. The control panel was 65 feet (20 m) long, or about the height of a six-story building. Yet the controls were so efficient that one person could control the entire operation. Each step of the lock operation had to be done in the correct order or it wouldn't work, so all the switches on the panel interlocked.

By 1911 the single set of locks at Pedro Miguel had been finished. The double set of locks at Miraflores and the triple set of locks at Gatun were finished in May 1913—six years after excavation of the lock sites had begun, and a year sooner than Goethals had antici-pated. Nothing else like these structures existed on earth. All that remained was to test them.

PREPARING FOR THE FUTURE

When the canal excavation was finished, Goethals started work on the buildings that would be needed to keep the canal running. Entrance terminals were built at each end of the canal. The commission expected thousands of ships to use the canal every year. To accommodate all the traffic, storehouses, dry docks, wharves, piers, and other docking facilities were also built.

Crude oil was just beginning to be used as fuel, but most ships and utilities used coal. Coal stations, heating plants, and fuel storage facilities were built throughout the zone. Warehouses to hold all the equipment needed to run the canal (such as cranes, shovels, and tractors) were also built.

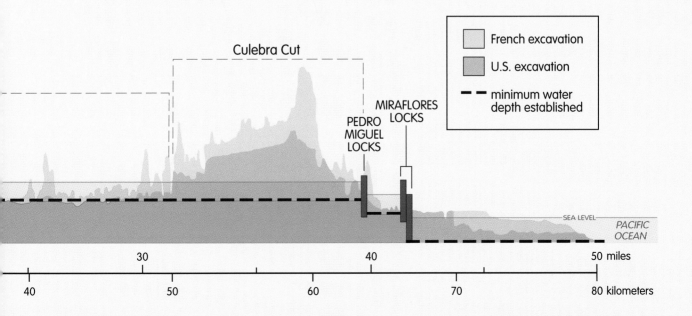

Chapter Seven
THE PANAMA CANAL
(1913–modern times)

Spectators cheered as the *Gatun*, a tugboat, passed through the Gatun Locks in September 1913.

As the Panama Canal neared completion, plans for defending it became as important as its actual construction. After a long debate about the canal's neutrality, Congress decided to fortify the canal against both sea and land attack.

Defending the canal had already been considered. Stevens and Goethals had located the locks at Miraflores rather than at the shoreline because both felt it would be impossible to defend shoreline locks from enemy bombardment.

Goethals also ordered the construction of several forts on both the Atlantic and Pacific sides. Soldiers would be stationed at the forts around the clock. Crews anchored antisubmarine mines in the water at both entrances to the canal. Nothing was done to defend against an air attack, since attack by air was not a possibility in this era.

By early 1913, all major canal projects were winding down. "Some of the concrete men had sunk to the level of laying sidewalks," one visitor noticed. Throughout the zone, excitement was in the air. People reported for work early and stayed late. They knew the end was approaching and wanted to be on hand to see the last load of earth scooped up by the last steam shovel.

That moment came in Culebra Cut on May 20, 1913. On that day, two steam shovels moved along the bottom of the cut from opposite ends. When they met, drivers Joseph S. Kirk and D. J. MacDonald got out, shook hands, and clapped each other on the back. Steam whistles blew, and thousands of watching workers and tourists cheered. The largest barrier was down.

THEY WORK

"I really believe that every American employed would have worked that year without pay . . . to see the first ship pass through the completed Canal," wrote Robert Wood, an army officer working in the zone. Their opportunity came on September 26, 1913, when an old tugboat named *Gatun* was sent through the triple locks at Gatun to see if they really worked. Goethals and thousands of spectators lined the banks of the locks and watched as the *Gatun,* decked out in colorful streamers and flags, made her way through the locks. It was a long, hot day, but when the *Gatun* finally made it through, the crowds along the banks went wild.

The locks not only worked—they worked perfectly. And in stark contrast to all the dirt, noise, and hubbub of construction, the locks were silent. The electric motors purred softly, the water gurgled quietly, and the great gates opened and closed with nary a click. The locks were a triumph in the technical and creative use of electricity, steel, concrete, and engineering principles.

The path between two oceans was about to become a reality. On October 13, 1913, President Woodrow Wilson pressed a small button in Washington, D.C. The signal zipped across telegraph wires to Panama. Seconds later, the temporary dam that had been holding back the Chagres River at Culebra Cut exploded in a cloud of dust. With a mighty roar, the river flooded into the canal—almost four hundred years to the day since Balboa had first spied the Pacific Ocean.

A SUBDUED MOMENT

It took several months for the entire canal to fill with water and for all the dredging to be finished. But with the bulk of the work done, thousands of employees began moving on to other jobs. Many went to the United States, especially to Detroit, Michigan, where the new automobile industry needed workers. Most of the Caribbean workers returned to their home islands, but some chose to stay in Panama.

Wilson disbanded the canal commission and appointed Goethals to be the first governor of the Panama Canal Zone. A newly organized Panama Canal Company would own, operate, and maintain the canal, workers' homes, utilities, warehouses, docking facilities, shops, and the Panama Railroad.

On January 7, 1914, the *Alexandre La Valley* did a test run through the canal, becoming the first ship to navigate it. Hardly anyone noticed that the *Alexandre La Valley* was a French crane boat that had been abandoned by Lesseps's canal company years earlier.

August 15, 1914, would be the day the canal officially opened for business. The United States had paid to build the canal, but Congress had ruled that the canal must break even financially when in operation. To pay for itself, the canal would charge ships a toll based on each ship's weight. Even U.S. ships would pay the toll.

A grand opening celebration would follow several months after the business opening. As part of the celebration, one hundred U.S. warships were scheduled to journey from the East Coast to Panama to transit the canal in a spectacular display of U.S. naval power. The ships would then continue to San Francisco, California, arriving in time for the opening of the Panama-Pacific International Exposition, a world's fair that documented the marvels of the new canal. A few days before the business opening in August, however, World War I broke out in Europe. The spectacular parade of warships never happened.

Opening day was quiet. Goethals anxiously watched from the banks as a cement carrier, the SS *Ancon,* became the Panama Canal's first official customer. But with Europe fast becoming a battlefield, the attention of other Americans was drawn away. The *New York Times* reported, "The Panama Canal is open to the commerce of the world. Henceforth ships may pass to

Goethals watches as the SS *Ancon* becomes the Panama Canal's first official customer in 1914.

and fro through that great waterway." But the story didn't make the front page. Instead, the single greatest undertaking the world had ever seen had become a back page event.

OPEN FOR BUSINESS

The full 9 miles (14 km) of Culebra Cut had been excavated at an enormous price. By the time the cut was complete, nearly 25 percent of all the dirt removed from the area had come from slides. The cost was $90 million, or $10 million per mile. David Gaillard, who had headed the work in the cut, suffered a nervous breakdown the summer after the cut was complete. Within a year, he was dead of a brain tumor. Culebra Cut was renamed Gaillard Cut in his honor.

Traffic was light during the first years of operation of the Panama Canal. By 1924, however, about five thousand ships were transiting the canal each year. Goethals had ordered that the vegetation be allowed to grow back all along the canal route. Travelers slipped along the nearly silent passageway, surrounded by green jungle and silvery blue water.

Maintenance problems and canal improvements were ongoing. Goethals had insisted the slides in Culebra Cut would stop once the cut was full of water, but he was wrong. In 1915 a slide closed the canal for more than six months. In 1974 one slide limited the canal to one-way traffic for months. And those were just two of the bigger slides over the years. In fact, more spoil has been removed since the canal has been open than was necessary for the original excavation.

Gatun Lake. By 1924 about five thousand ships were using the Panama Canal each year.

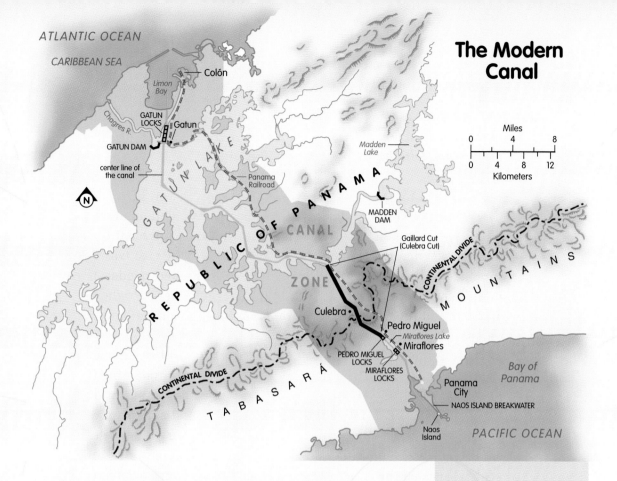

The Modern Canal

ATLANTIC OCEAN

CARIBBEAN SEA

Colón

Limon Bay

GATUN LOCKS

Gatun

GATUN DAM

center line of the canal

Chagres R.

Panama Railroad

GATUN LAKE

Madden Lake

MADDEN DAM

CANAL

Gaillard Cut (Culebra Cut)

CONTINENTAL DIVIDE

ZONE

Culebra

MOUNTAINS

Pedro Miguel

Miraflores Lake

Miraflores

PEDRO MIGUEL LOCKS

MIRAFLORES LOCKS

Bay of Panama

Panama City

NAOS ISLAND BREAKWATER

Naos Island

PACIFIC OCEAN

REPUBLIC OF PANAMA

CONTINENTAL DIVIDE

TABASARÁ

N

Miles
0   4   8
0   4   8   12
Kilometers

When the Madden Dam was constructed, it created a 22-square-mile (57-square-kilometer) lake. It further controls the Chagres River and produces extra power for the zone.

For decades the canal's capacity was and continues to be severely stretched. In 1940 excavation started on a third set of locks that would be 140 feet (43 m) wide and 1,200 feet (366 m) long. But the work stopped when the United States entered World War II in 1941, and never resumed.

Channel lighting was added in 1966 so the canal could be used twenty-four hours a day. Other modern inventions have been added over the years, such as closed-circuit TV, high-frequency radios, and computers.

Gaillard Cut always required more maintenance than any other part of the canal. In January 1992, the Panama Canal Company started a renovation project to make the Gaillard Cut safer. The work is divided into two areas: dry excavation and wet excavation. The dry excavation widens the cut and reduces the steepness of the sides. The wet excavation deepens the cut so larger ships can navigate more safely. Like the original excavation of the cut, these renovations require extensive blasting with dynamite.

Madden Lake was created in 1935 when Madden Dam was built.

A LASTING LEGACY...

In modern times, more than fifteen thousand ships transit the Panama Canal each year. But the canal's contribution extends beyond its role as a world highway. Because the canal project was unlike anything the world had ever seen, the builders discovered as they went along that many accepted procedures simply didn't work in Panama. They had to develop new techniques to get the project completed. In the nine years it took to build the canal, more advances occurred in the fields of medicine, electricity, hydroelectric power, and engineering than ever before in history.

The field of medicine probably benefited the most. Prior to Gorgas's work with yellow fever and malaria, thousands of people died from these diseases. Gorgas's work opened up new doors in the field of tropical diseases and prompted the development of many new medicines.

Electricity was barely known when the canal project started. Thanks to the decision to make the canal electric, the entire field of electrical engineering benefited. Techniques pioneered at the Panama Canal helped electrify cities and villages around the world.

Other fields, such as geologic and hydraulic engineering, benefited from the inventions and new techniques needed just to excavate Culebra Cut. The construction of the locks yielded more breakthroughs. For example, the valves and gears in the locks had to be specially designed and manufactured. The canal's innovative designs advanced not only American technology but also

The Panama Canal's many resourceful engineers helped make its innovations possible.

Gatun Locks. The design of the locks allows ships traveling in opposite directions to pass through the canal at the same time.

American manufacturing. Nearly one hundred years after their construction, the locks of the Panama Canal remain in near-perfect condition.

. . . AND AN INDEPENDENT PANAMA

Despite the positive advances, the canal's legacy has not been all positive. Roosevelt's gunboat diplomacy during Panama's quest for independence created ill feelings almost immediately. Most Panamanians were outraged when they discovered what had happened through the Hay-Bunau-Varilla Treaty, with nearly one-third of their country given to a foreign nation to do with as it pleased. Nearly every country in Latin America joined Panama in believing that the United States had no right to meddle in Latin American affairs.

The passage of time did not diminish resentment for many Panamanians. The riots of 1912 and 1915 were followed by riots in 1947, 1958, 1959, 1962, 1964, 1968, 1987, and into the 1990s. Pana-manians and U.S. citizens were killed in nearly every riot. All of the riots were started by Panamanians, and most occurred

PAYING FOR THE CANAL

By law, the Panama Canal must break even financially. To ensure that the canal pays its expenses, a toll system was set up right from the start. The first tolls, established by Congress in 1914, were set at $.90 per cargo ton. The tolls remained at this level until 1973. The Panama Canal Company suffered its first financial loss in that year. Consequently, the tolls were raised in 1974 to $1.08 per cargo ton. Since then, the tolls have been raised several more times. The *Radiance of the Seas* paid $202,176.76 to transit the canal in April 2001. The lowest toll ever paid came from Richard Halliburton, an adventurer who paid $.36 in 1928 to swim through the canal.

GETTING THROUGH THE CANAL

No ship may transit the canal on its own. Ships cannot use their own captains in the canal. Frequently, they don't even use their own engines. As soon as a ship arrives at either entrance to the canal, a special canal captain boards the ship and takes command. He or she is in charge of navigating the ship through the sea channels and inland channels. Having special canal captains keeps inexperienced ship captains from accidentally damaging the canal. Even so, accidents occur about every nine days.

At the locks, the ship is attached to "mules" with cables. Mules are small engines that look like miniature railroad locomotives. They run on tracks alongside the locks. They pull the ship through each lock. Approximately eight mules (four on each side of the ship) are used at each lock.

The canal captain remains in charge until the ship exits the canal. Transit time is usually about fifteen hours. Only a little more than half this time is spent moving. The rest is spent waiting in line.

because Panamanians felt that U.S. citizens should not be controlling a section of their country.

The Hay-Bunau-Varilla Treaty was renegotiated in 1936 and again in 1955 to give Panama more sovereignty in the zone. The changes to the treaty included seemingly small but important issues, such as the decision to fly both the U.S. flag and the Panamanian flag in the zone. Annual payments for use of the zone were increased. Hiring practices and salaries for Panamanians working in the zone were improved.

In the 1970s, U.S. president Jimmy Carter and others devoted years of effort to developing an entirely new treaty. On September 7, 1977, following the second longest treaty debate in U.S. history, the Panama Canal Treaty was ratified. It spelled out a plan to

gradually give full control of the zone to Panama over a period of twenty years. In a second treaty, the Neutrality Treaty, Panama and the United States guaranteed that all nations are guaranteed equal access and tolls. The canal will always remain neutral.

The Panama Canal Treaty went into effect on October 1, 1979. The Panama Canal Zone government and the Panama Canal Company disbanded. Panama took possession of 65 percent of the land in the zone and all of the railroad. And all shops, warehouses, and fueling facilities were given to Panama. By the time the Panama Canal Treaty expired on December 31, 1999, Panama alone had the authority to operate the Panama Canal and to maintain military operations in Panama. The United States has retained the right to use military force to defend the canal.

U.S. soldiers lower the flag at the Panama Canal in 1999. The nation of Panama took control of the canal that December.

WHAT NEXT?

Since the canal opened, bigger and bigger ships have been built. Many of them are too large to navigate the canal. Channels can be cut deeper and wider, but the size of the concrete locks is set. Many nations, including the United States, talk about building a new canal at a second location in Latin America—perhaps in Nicaragua or in Mexico. So far, another canal remains a dream. But no matter what the future brings, the Panama Canal will always remain a great building feat. It is an amazing passageway that not only links two oceans but also links the past with the present. From Balboa's first siting of the Pacific to the *Alexandre La Valley*'s first transit, the canal is a living monument to the perseverance, dedication, and courage of thousands of people. Nothing—not even another canal—will ever take away the glory of the Panama Canal.

A Timeline of the Panama Canal

1502 Christopher Columbus explores Panama.

1513 Vasco Nuñez de Balboa and his crew cross the Isthmus of Panama, becoming the first Europeans to prove that only a narrow strip of land separates the Atlantic and Pacific Oceans there.

1534 Holy Roman Emperor Charles V orders a study of possible canal routes in Panama.

1850 The discovery of gold in California brings a deluge of would-be prospectors to Panama. After construction began on the Panama Railroad in 1850, it became one link in the fastest route from the East Coast to the West Coast.

1876 A U.S. commission recommends a Nicaragua route for a canal.

1879 The French Committee for Cutting the Interoceanic Canal is formed.

1880 Ferdinand de Lesseps arrives in Panama.

1881 De Lesseps and his company buy the rights to the Panama Railroad. The first French employee to die of yellow fever is buried.

1882 An earthquake in Panama creates mud slides in Culebra Cut.

This cross section shows the Isthmus of Panama before humans tried to build a canal there.

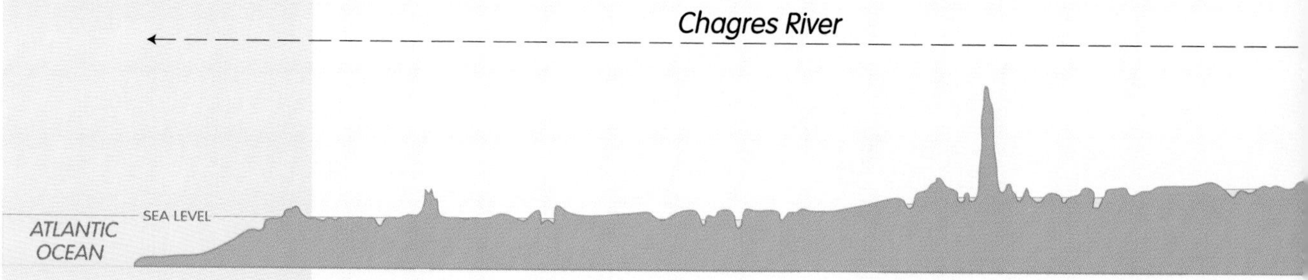

Chagres River

SEA LEVEL

ATLANTIC
OCEAN

1884 The French employ more than nineteen thousand laborers on the canal.

1885 One-tenth of the excavation at Culebra Cut is complete.

1887 The French company agrees to abandon the plan for a sea-level canal.

1888 Construction on a new plan for a lock canal begins. Thousands of French workers are buried in Panama graveyards, having died of yellow fever, malaria, and other causes.

1889 The French company runs out of money. Most work on the canal stops.

1894 Ferdinand de Lesseps and his son, Charles, are indicted for fraud. Although both are found guilty, neither is required to go to jail.

1898 French investors actively seek a buyer for the canal project. The battleship *Maine,* stationed in Cuba, blows up, drawing the United States into the Spanish-American War. The *Oregon* sets out for Cuba from the West Coast, steaming around South America and arriving in Cuba sixty-seven days later.

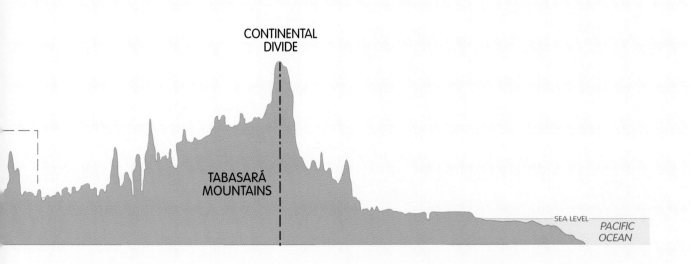

1899 U.S. president William McKinley hears a report on a Nicaragua route for a canal.

1901 McKinley is assassinated, and Theodore Roosevelt becomes U.S. president.

1902 Philippe Bunau-Varilla journeys to the United States and tries to sell the French assets in Panama. President Roosevelt decides he wants to buy the assets and asks Congress to approve the Panama route.

1903 Panama rebels against Colombia. Roosevelt sends U.S. warships to the isthmus in support of the Panamanian revolution. Panama wins independence within a few days.

1903 In December the Hay-Bunau-Varilla Treaty is signed, giving the United States the right to build a canal through a 10-mile-wide (16-km-wide) zone in the middle of Panama.

1904 U.S. construction begins. John Findley Wallace serves as chief engineer.

1905 John Frank Stevens serves as chief engineer. Dr. William Gorgas leads a campaign against tropical disease and eradicates yellow fever in Panama.

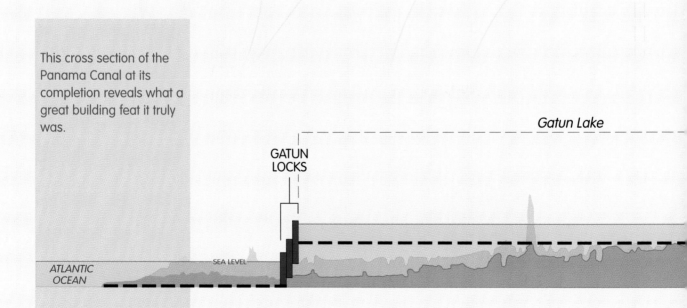

This cross section of the Panama Canal at its completion reveals what a great building feat it truly was.

Gatun Lake

GATUN
LOCKS

SEA LEVEL

*ATLANTIC
OCEAN*

1906 Roosevelt visits Panama.

1907 George Washington Goethals becomes chief engineer. He is responsible only to the U.S. president and U.S. secretary of war. Construction on the Panama Canal locks begins.

1908 A record-high amount of spoil is removed from Culebra Cut. Relocation of the Panama Railroad to higher ground begins.

1911 The Pedro Miguel Locks are completed.

1913 The Miraflores Locks and the Gatun Locks are completed. In September the Gatun Locks get their first test when the tugboat *Gatun* sails through them.

1914 The *Alexandre La xlley* becomes the first vessel to completely transit the canal.

1979 The Panama Canal Treaty, negotiated by the United States and the Republic of Panama, goes into force. It will gradually shift control of the canal to Panama. It calls for a transition period of twenty years.

1999 On December 31, authority over the canal is fully transferred to Panama.

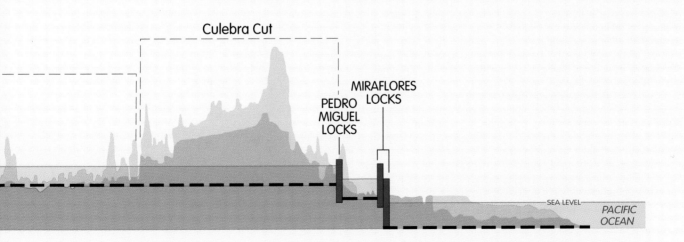

Source Notes

Acknowledgments for quoted material: p. 8, *Nation,* November 23, 1905; p. 12, as quoted in Tim McNeese, *The Panama Canal* (San Diego, CA: Lucent Books, 1997); pp. 12, 13, Willis Fletcher Johnson, *Four Centuries of the Panama Canal* (New York: Henry Holt, 1906); pp. 16, 18, 22, 36, 37, 38, 42, 44, 45, 46, 53, 55, 59, 79, as quoted in David McCullough, *The Path between the Seas* (New York: Simon and Schuster, 1977); pp. 25, 46, 47, 49, 50, 53, Arthur Bullard, *The Canal, the Country, the People* (New York: Macmillan, 1914); p. 28, Miles P. DuVal Jr., *And the Mountains Will Move: The Story of the Building of the Panama Canal* (Palo Alto, CA: Stanford University Press, 1947); p. 43, Howard Copeland Hill, *Roosevelt and the Caribbean* (Chicago: University of Chicago Press, 1927); pp. 32, 51, 56, 64, as quoted in Judith St. George, *Panama Canal: Gateway to the World* (New York: G. P. Putnam's Sons, 1989); p. 52, as quoted in Helen Nicolay, *The Bridge of Water: The Story of Panama and the Canal* (New York: D. Appleton-Century, 1940); p. 81, *New York Tribune,* September 28, 1882.

Selected Bibliography

Conniff, Michael L. *Panama and the United States: The Forced Alliance.* Athens, GA: University of Georgia Press, 1992.

Lee, W. Storrs. *The Strength to Move a Mountain.* New York: G. P. Putnam's Sons, 1958.

LeFeber, Walter. *The Panama Canal: The Crisis in Historical Perspective.* New York: Oxford University Press, 1978.

Lindop, Edmund. *Panama and the United States: Divided by the Canal.* New York: Twenty-First Century Books/Henry Holt and Co., 1997.

McCullough, David. *The Path between the Seas.* New York: Simon and Schuster, 1977.

Panama Canal Authority. "Gaillard Cut Widening Progam." *The Panama Canal.* N.d. <http://www.pancanal.com> (summer 2001).

Ryan, Paul B. *The Panama Canal Controversy.* Stanford, CA: Hoover Institution Press, 1977.

Further Reading

Brown, Patrice C. "Prologue: The Panama Canal: The African American Experience." *National Archives and Records Administration.*
<http://www.nara.gov/publications/prologue/panama.html>
This article discusses the treatment of African American canal workers. Advanced students will find many primary sources on the canal catalogued at NARA's online site.

CIA. *The World Factbook.*
<http://www.odci.gov/cia/publications/factbook/>
Find a map, geography information, and statistics about the Republic of Panama by clicking on "Panama." Country information is updated every year.

CZ Brats
<http://www.czbrats.com>
This site is maintained and regularly updated by people who grew up in the canal zone. Searching on "Builders of the Panama Canal" leads to treasures such as documents written by the canal's chief engineers; letters and speeches of President Theodore Roosevelt; and memorabilia such as "Panama Roughneck Ballads," written in 1912 by Panama resident John Hall.

McNeese, Tim. *The Panama Canal.* **San Diego, CA: Lucent Books, 1997.**
This readable book on the history of the Panama Canal is geared for upper-elementary-age readers.

Panama Canal Authority. *The Panama Canal.*
<http://www.pancanal.com/>
Newsworthy events and current developments are covered on this site in both Spanish and English. Of special interest is a camera shot of live action at the canal. Online visitors can even request a new camera angle.

Panama Canal History Museum. *canalmuseum.com*
<http://www.canalmuseum.com>
Photos, documents, stories, books, and links are available on this extensive site.

St. George, Judith. *Panama Canal: Gateway to the World.* **New York: G. P. Putnam's Sons, 1989.**
Young readers will find the overview in this book useful for reports.

Smithsonian Institution Libraries. *Make the Dirt Fly!*
<http://www.sil.si.edu/Exhibitions/Make-the-Dirt-Fly/>
The Smithsonian's online exhibit of the building of the Panama Canal features a fact-filled text and many quotes. Artifacts such as postcards published during canal construction enliven the site.

Index

Lesley A. DuTemple has written more than a dozen books for young readers, including many award-winning titles such as her biography *Jacques Cousteau,* winner of the National Science Teachers Association/Children's Book Council Outstanding Science Trade Books for Children. After graduating from the University of California, San Diego, she attended the University of Utah's Graduate School of Architecture, where she concentrated in design and architectural history. The creator of the **Great Building Feats** series, she believes, "There's a human story behind every one of these building feats, and those stories are just as amazing as the projects themselves."

Photo Acknowledgments

All attempts have been made to contact the copyright holder(s) of the images in this book. If your image appears without proper credit, please contact Lerner Publishing Group.

The images in this book are used with the permission of: Brown Brothers, pp. 1, 20, 24, 26 (inset), 26–27, 32, 34–35, 36, 37, 38, 39 (top), 47, 48 (inset), 48–49, 50, 56–57, 61, 62, 64, 80, 81, 82, 85; Library of Congress, pp. 2–3, 30–31, 52, 53, 65, 66 (inset), 66–67; Hulton | Archive/Getty Images, pp. 4 (inset), 4–5, 8, 15, 16, 44, 70, 76, 78–79, 87; © Bettmann/CORBIS, pp. 8–9 10, 14, 19 (© CORBIS), 28 (© CORBIS), 59, 75 (© CORBIS); IPS, pp. 17, 41 (both), 74; Culver Pictures, pp. 21, 58; National Archives, pp. 22, 40; J. W. D. Collins, p. 39 (bottom), 46; © AFP/CORBIS, pp. 51, 73; Panama Canal Museum, pp. 55, 71, 84; © Catherine Gehm, p. 86. Maps and diagrams by Laura Westlund, pp. 6, 12, 24–25, 29, 33, 54–55, 69, 76–77, 88–89, 90–91.

Cover photos are by Panama Canal Museum (front) and Brown Brothers (back).